THE CHURCH OF SANTA TRINITA
IN FLORENCE

MONOGRAPHS ON ARCHAEOLOGY AND FINE ARTS

SPONSORED BY

THE ARCHAEOLOGICAL INSTITUTE OF AMERICA AND

THE COLLEGE ART ASSOCIATION OF AMERICA

XII

THE CHURCH OF SANTA TRINITA
IN FLORENCE

BY

HOWARD SAALMAN

Carnegie Institute of Technology

Pittsburgh, Pennsylvania

ST. JOSEPH'S UNIVERSITY
NA5621.S37S2
The Church of Santa Trinita in Florence.

3 9353 00143 0600

Folio
NA
5621
.S37
S2

1966

PUBLISHED BY THE COLLEGE ART ASSOCIATION OF AMERICA

IN CONJUNCTION WITH THE ART BULLETIN

H. W. Janson, Editor

150990

The publication of this monograph
has been aided by a grant from the
Samuel H. Kress Foundation

❖

Copyright 1966
by College Art Association
All Rights Reserved
L.C. Card No. 66-27568

PREFACE

THIS study was carried out during a two-year period of research in Italy, 1956-1958, supported by a Fulbright Fellowship. The work was aided by supplementary grants from New York University and the Phyllis Lambert Architectural Research and Publication Fund directed by Professor Richard Krautheimer.

An earlier version of this report was accepted in October 1960 by the faculty of the Institute of Fine Arts, New York University, in partial fulfilment of the requirements for the degree of Doctor of Philosophy.

The manuscript benefited materially from a critical review by Dr. Friedrich Oswald, then at the Kunsthistorisches Institut in Florence (1961). His observations led me to alter my initial interpretations in several important respects. I am grateful to him for his interest and advice and specific reference to his contributions will be made in the notes where appropriate.

The permission to carry out the necessary excavations was granted by Dott. Alfredo Barbacci, then Soprintendente ai Monumenti delle Provincie di Firenze, Arezzo e Pistoia, through the interest and cooperation of the present Soprintendente, Arch. Guido Morozzi. My collaborator, Mrs. Phyllis Dearborn Massar, gave generously of her time and talent in executing the photographs for Figs. 2, 5, 6, 7, 8 and 11.

Dott. Berta Leggeri, Florence, prepared the plans of the excavation and produced the measured survey of the church. Messrs. R. Pagliero, G. Sixta, R. Singh, A. El Mously and Miss S. Abigadol, Department of Architecture, Carnegie Institute of Technology as well as Mr. A. Frazer, Poughkeepsie, were helpful in the revision of the plans. Mr. David Eisenhauer, Stockholm, assisted in a final revision of the plans and executed additional drawings.

A word of warm appreciation must go to Professor Ulrich Middeldorf, Director of the Kunsthistorisches Institut, Florence, for his personal assistance on many occasions and to the members of his staff for their continuous interest and cooperation.

To the tireless editor of this series, Professor Horst W. Janson, go the author's thanks for his unfailingly prompt and expert advice and assistance in the final preparation of the text and the figures.

H.S.

I Tatti, Florence
July, 1964

TABLE OF CONTENTS

THE CHURCH OF SANTA TRINITA
IN FLORENCE

BACKGROUND: THE VASARI TRADITION

DATES, DOCUMENTS AND SOURCES

WHEN the present church of Santa Trinita in Florence (Pls. I, III, Figs. 2, 5-8) was built, it took the place of a preceding church. Little else regarding the history of this building is certain. Vasari, casting about for a date and attribution for the existing church, stated flatly that it was built by Nicola Pisano "in the year the Guelfs came back to Florence."[1] According to Giovanni Villani, who, however, does not mention either the church or Nicola Pisano, this event can be fixed in the year 1250-1251.[2] Considering that we have no documented architectural works by Nicola Pisano, and considering, further, the predominantly fourteenth century character of the present church, this date and attribution would seem at first glance to deserve no more than an attempt to explain it. But Vasari's suggestion has had a long and checkered history.

The next attempt to define the history of the building is due to the Abbot Averardo Niccolini. In an inventory report to his Roman superior sent off in 1650, he set down the results of his historical research which he recopied into a manuscript of 1661 now in the Florentine archives.[3] Niccolini, basing himself on some archival material and "la crononica [sic] affissa nella nostra chiesa alla capella della Pietà" presented five dates: 800, 1222, 1227, 1250 and 1327. Santa Trinita, he reports, was one of twelve collegiate churches in Florence founded in 800 or 810 by Charlemagne. According to a now lost "Libro di Ricordanze in Ripoli, segn. AO a carte 68," Pope Gregory IX made a dedication at the church on September 27, 1222. The "crononica" stated that Gregory IX granted "l'uso dei pontificiali . . . l'anno 1227, terzo del suo pontificato." Niccolini doubted the accuracy of this report, probably in part because 1227 was actually the year of Gregory IX's elevation and in part because other records report the granting of the "pontificiali" much later, in the fifteenth century.[4] Obviously basing himself on Vasari, Niccolini then related that "fu restaurata questa [chiesa] nell'anno 1250. Fu dato il disegnio di questo tempio da Nicola Pisano e condotta a fine acconciamente come si vede."[5]

Giamboni in his *Diario sacro*,[6] indicates that Gregory's dedication should be dated December 27, 1227 because December 27 marks the annual *festa principale* of the church. An entry in the notes of Senator Carlo Strozzi[7] gives the date December 27, 1237, possible since Gregory reigned until 1241. The date 1237 is repeated by Richa[8] who added the information, gleaned from Giamboni, that Gregory IX granted a plenary indulgence to the church.

Two other dates belong in this discussion: 1257 and/or 1258. Senator Strozzi reports in several places in his notes about a piece of marble, apparently round, with an *abaco*, i.e., a monogrammatic inscription, forming the number "MCCLVIII." In one place Strozzi states that the *abaco* is "al

1. G. Vasari, *Le vite de' più eccellenti pittori ed architettori*, G. Milanesi, ed., Florence, 1878-1885, I, p. 303; *idem*, K. Frey, ed., Munich, 1911, I, p. 666. Cf. also pp. 575, 824f.

2. G. Villani, *Cronica*, ed. Sansoni, Florence, 1844, VI, 42: January 7, 1250, i.e., 1251 *stile comune*.

3. C. Botto, "Note e documenti sulla chiesa di S. Trinita in Firenze," *Rivista d'Arte*, XX, 1938, pp. 2-4. Hereafter, Botto, 1938.

4. G. Richa, *Notizie istoriche delle chiese fiorentine*, Florence, 1755, III, pp. 149-150; D. M. Manni, *Osservazioni istoriche . . . sopra sigilli antichi de' secoli bassi*, Florence, 1743, XIV, p. 24. Hereafter, Richa, *Chiese*.

5. C. Botto, 1938, pp. 2-4.

6. L. A. Giamboni, *Diario sacro e guida perpetua*, Florence, 1700, p. 284.

7. W. and E. Paatz, *Die Kirchen von Florenz*, Frankfort on the Main, 1940-1955, V, p. 320 n. 10. Hereafter, Paatz (followed by Vol. No.). This notice was reported by H. Siebenhuener (Arch. di Stato, Firenze, *Carte Strozziane, Repert. eccl.* 554 B. 112).

8. G. Richa, *Chiese*, III, p. 149: dedication, December 27, 1237 ". . . giusta il Sig. Manni, il Giamboni, e la tradizione del Monastero. . . ." Since Richa could find no notice of Gregory IX in Florence in the years around 1237 in Villani or L'Ammirato, he added: ". . . convien dire, che da lui fosse fatta questa consecrazione negli anni, che fu egli Legato in Toscana, colla quale dignità trovasi appellato nelle memorie de' Capitoli generali di Vallombrosa *Preside D. Ugolino Card. Ostien. in partibus Tuscie Legato*, nel qual caso sarebbe di uopo correggere il millesimo." Giamboni (*op.cit.*, p. 284), however, gave the date 1227.

fianco" of the church;[9] elsewhere it is "sopra la porta."[10] Both may be correct. Richa refers to a "tondo di marmo come un'ostia con lettere . . . accanto alla porta di mezzo," but reads the date as "MCCLVII," probably an error after Strozzi.[11] All agree that the plaque was removed when Buontalenti built the present façade after 1592. The "tondo" was apparently too small a detail to be included in the view of the façade as it was until its demolition after 1592, represented in the fresco by Domenico Ghirlandaio in the Sassetti Chapel in Santa Trinita (Fig. 3).

There is finally another date reported by Niccolini, the year 1327: another consecration, by Pope John XXII.

Summing up, we have the following dates: 800/810 (Niccolini); September 27, 1222 (Niccolini-Ripoli archives); 1227 (Niccolini-"crononica"); December 27, 1227 (Giamboni); December 27, 1237 (Strozzi-Richa); 1250-51 (Vasari-Niccolini); 1257 or 1258 (Strozzi-Richa); 1327 (Niccolini-"crononica").

Only a few other points of chronological reference are available: The church is first mentioned in a document of 1077.[12] The Vallombrosians took possession of it in 1092.[13] A document of 1124 refers to a *casa solariata . . . iuxta ecclesiam Sancte Trinitatis.*[14] In 1178 the church received the *jus parrochiale*, a few years after it was enclosed in the expanded city wall. The parish was enlarged a few years later.[15] In 1277, the monks bought some houses in the Via Parione to build a hospital.[16] Cimabue painted his great Madonna for Santa Trinita around 1285.[17] Meetings were held in the church in 1289 and 1301.[18] A later-demolished chapel of Saints James and Benedict is mentioned in a document of 1318. Its location is not identified.[19] Dino Compagni, the Florentine chronicler and politician was reportedly buried in the still-existing fourth chapel on the left side of the church in 1324.[20] A seventeenth century inscription in the first left-hand chapel (Strozzi) declares that the chapel was *extructum* in 1340.[21] There is ample documentation of an extensive rebuilding of the church beginning around 1360, rebuilding which goes far beyond simple "repairs."[22]

NINETEENTH CENTURY RESTORATIONS AND DISCOVERIES

After the construction of the sacristy in the fifteenth century[22a] and two small chapels at the southern end of the transept in the early sixteenth century, the only major addition to the existing church was the impressive exterior façade built by Buontalenti in 1592.[23]

9. Florence, Bibl. Nazionale, Cod. Strozziano IX, 127, fol. 111 (reported by Gronau).

10. Arch. di St., Firenze, *Carte Strozziane, Repert. eccl.* 555, +B. 111: "Sopra la Porta di detta Chiesa eragia in un pezzetto d'Marmo queste figure d'Abbacco MCCLVIII, che fu levato l'anno 1594 con l'Occasione di rifare la Facciata."

11. G. Richa, *Chiese*, III, p. 143: ". . . accanto alla porta di mezzo, innanzi che fosse rinnovata di pietre, vedevosi un tondo di marmo come un'ostia con lettere, che formavano il seguente millesimo: MCCLVII."

12. A. Cocchi, *Le chiese di Firenze*, Florence, 1903, I, pp. 167f.: an act is notarized . . . *foras muros florentie civitatis prope ecclesiam sancte trinitatis* . . . (Arch. di St., Firenze, *Diplomatico*, Badia a Ripoli, 1077, 19 luglio).

13. Cf. Paatz V, p. 319 n. 7; Botto, 1938, p. 2.

14. R. Davidsohn, *Geschichte von Florenz*, I, Berlin, 1896f., p. 731 n. 1; cf. also R. Piattoli, ed., *Regesta chartarum Italiae. XXIII. Le carte della Canonica della Cattedrale di Firenze (723-1149)*, Rome, 1938, pp. 408f., doc. 169.

15. Documents: Botto, 1938, p. 2 n. 3.

16. D. M. Manni, *Sigilli antichi*, XIV, p. 20. Cf. R. Baldaccini, "S. Trinita nel periodo gotico," *Rivista d'Arte*, XXVII, 1951-1952, p. 49 n. 6. Hereafter, Baldaccini, 1951-1952.

17. For a discussion of the attribution and the date, cf. Paatz V, p. 383 n. 382. Prof. Wolfgang Lotz has suggested orally that iconographical reasons lead him to suspect that

the Cimabue Madonna was not planned for the main altar of Santa Trinita.

18. Richa, *Chiese*, III, pp. 141-142.

19. Cf. Botto, 1938, p. 13. Botto cites a different dedication for the chapel: SS. Filippo e Jacopo. So still Paatz V, p. 259. The document of 1318 (Arch. di St., Firenze, *Conventi*, 224, Fa. 222, c. 170, doc. 70) which survives in a 17th century copy, actually reads *Cappella Sanctorum Jacobi et Benedicti.*

20. Richa, *Chiese*, III, p. 165. Cf. Paatz V, p. 322 n. 18. Unpublished research by Dr. Friedrich Oswald suggests that Compagni may not have been buried here in 1324 as generally believed, since the chapel apparently did not pass into possession of the Compagni family until 1434.

21. Cf. A. Cocchi, *Le chiese di Firenze*, Florence, 1903, p. 188, hereafter, Cocchi, *Chiese*; Richa, *Chiese*, III, p. 164; Paatz V, p. 377 n. 309. According to Richa (III, p. 161), the chapel was originally the property of the Carducci and was inherited by the Strozzi in the 15th century.

22. Cited in part by G. Carocci, "A proposito dei restauri di S. Trinita," *Arte e Storia*, III, 1884, pp. 251f.; E. Marcucci, "Restauri di S. Trinita," *Arte e Storia*, IV, 1885, pp. 74f. *In extenso*: Botto, 1938. Cf. also Paatz V, pp. 328f. nn. 40f.

22a. Cf. H. Saalman, "The Palazzo Comunale in Montepulciano," *Zeitschrift für Kunstgeschichte*, XXVIII, 1965, pp. 5ff.

23. Paatz V, pp. 262, 336 n. 85.

From 1881 to 1897 the church underwent a restoration during which some Baroque accretions were destroyed or removed.[24] After this face-lifting the interior appearance of the building approximated its pre-sixteenth century state, but a number of arbitrary elements had been added, e.g., the horizontal strips articulating the piers and the upper oculus in the interior façade wall (Figs. 78-80).[25] The insertion of this oculus apparently led to the discovery that the interior façade wall contained parts of an older smaller church.[26] Though composed of several unhomogeneous parts (cf. pp. 23f. below), this wall has generally been considered to be *in toto* the interior façade of an eleventh century church on the site. It was left exposed after the restoration (Figs. 8, 9, 10, 43).

The pavement of the church had been raised 40cm in 1820 after repeated flooding of the building. With the danger of flooding largely eliminated after the construction of the present high Arno embankments in the middle of the nineteenth century, the pavement was restored to its present level in the 1880's.

A tomb excavation in 1820 had led to the rediscovery of a substructure below the fourth bay of the southern (left-hand) aisle. In 1885-1887 this area was explored. A trefoil structure extending across the nave with an apparent level 2.97m under the present pavement with windows respectively 1.71 and 1.78m above the —2.97m level came to light.[27] At a point 1.49m above the lower level, 1.48m under the present pavement and directly adjoining the trilobe structure, the cut-off stumps of two trefoil piers, evidently related to the interior façade laid bare at this time, were unearthed. The piers are built up of blocks of *verde di Prato* and are very similar to piers in San Miniato and other eleventh century churches in Florence. The existence of colonettes and their bases indicate that the trefoil substructure had served as a hall crypt at some time. It is generally referred to as the "crypt." This underground complex was restored, revaulted and made accessible by a modern set of narrow steps leading down from the fourth nave bay (Pls. III, IV, Figs. 11-23). No detailed excavation report, drawings or photographs were published.[28]

---

24. The controversies surrounding this restoration are chronicled in the artistic journals of the period. Cf. particularly Guido Carocci's *Arte e Storia* in the years 1881ff. Cf. also P. Franceschini, *Il nuovo osservatore fiorentino*, 1885f., p. 45; *idem, Del restauro al tempio di S. Trinita in Firenze*, Florence, 1898; Don F. Tarani, *Cenni storichi e artistichi della chiesa di S. Trinita e suo restauro*, Florence, 1897. For Castellazzi's idea of what should be done, including a recomposition of the "Gothic" façade, cf. G. Castellazzi, *La basilica di S. Trinita, i suoi tempi e il suo restauro*, Florence, 1887, plate facing p. 33. A key document in this connection is the report made by a special committee of experts set up in the wake of criticisms of the restorer Castellazzi's plans: G. Poggi, G. Milanesi, L. Del Moro and E. Marcucci, *Intorno al progetto di restauro della chiesa di S. Trinita, presentato dal Prof. Comm. Giuseppe Castellazzi. Relazione della Sotto-Commissione di Vigilanza alla Commissione Consultiva Conservatrice di Belle Arti per la Provincia di Firenze*, Florence, June, 1885. The recommendations of the subcommission of 1885 were followed in full. The full history of the restoration is documented in the *pratiche* of the Florentine *Prefettura* preserved in the Archivio di Stato (cf. note 25 infra).

25. Dr. F. Oswald found Castellazzi's preliminary report and plans of 1885 in the archives of the Soprintendenza ai Monumenti and the Archivio di Stato, Florence (ASF, Prefettura di Firenze, 1890, Filza 64[I] and 64[II], Serie 1, Categ. 16. Istruzione 39. Belle Arti, Chiesa di Santa Trinita, Lavori) in Florence in the spring of 1961. Neither the drawings nor the written report throw much additional light on the question of the previous state of the building with one important exception. It appears that the upper of the two round windows visible on the façade interior is a product of Commendatore Castellazzi's imagination, evidently intended to let more light into the nave. On the horizontal strips, cf. note 181 infra.

26. G. Carocci, *Arte e Storia*, VII, 1887, pp. 7, 16.

27. G. Carocci, *Arte e Storia*, VII, 1888, pp. 50, 64.

28. Among the drawings (Figs. 78-80) in the archives of the Soprintendenza ai Monumenti in Florence there is a curiously inadequate rendering of the "crypt" together with a hypothetical reconstruction of the plan of Trinita II, apparently made at the time of the reconstruction work in 1887-1888 carried out under the aegis of the "Sottocommissione di Vigilanza" composed of Poggi, Milanesi and Del Moro. Whether the square foundations (?) marking the bays of Trinita II are based on excavations in the nave (which was then still without its modern pavement), is unclear. A survey of the restoration documents during these years (cf. note 25) indicates that in the rush to finish up the long-drawn-out affair the restorers spent little time in making careful archaeological studies.

CHAPTER II

RECENT STUDIES
AND EXCAVATIONS—1957-1958

SINCE the restorations of 1885-1897, some or all of the recognized structures presently or formerly on the site of Santa Trinita have received attention. Three more recent authors, Botto,[29] Paatz[30] and Baldaccini[31] have dealt with the complex in detail. The present writer returned to the problem in the summer of 1957, prompted by some unanswered questions and the opportunity offered by repair work in the "crypt."

The studies comprised test excavations in October, 1957 and a more extensive campaign of excavations in February-March, 1958. The results, while leaving some questions pending, have given an entirely new face to the problem. The purpose of this monograph is to present a detailed report of these excavations and to summarize their significance for the successive building periods.

GENERAL PROBLEMS

Some problems encountered in the excavations may be mentioned briefly. Directly under the brick pavement consisting of roughly 10 x 25cm brick *quadroni*, laid in a herringbone pattern when the original church level was restored in the 1880's, a roughly 40cm deep footing of river stones lies on a 25cm deep layer of dry fill. Below this a layer of hard, tightly packed red clay fill mixed with stone, glass, metal and pottery fragments extends to a depth of about 3m (equivalent to the river level less than 75m away). These fragments date from all periods, but appear to be largely of the seventeenth, eighteenth and nineteenth centuries. Relatively few areas under the church can be considered as untouched since burials continued in all parts of the church until the early nineteenth century. Except in the chapels, the graves are no longer marked, for all tombstones in the pavement of the nave and aisles were removed around 1820 when the pavement was raised, but tombs are ubiquitous throughout the aisles and transept. With a few exceptions, the tombs were filled in around 1820 or when the pavement was lowered in the 1880's. Mostly dating from the seventeenth or eighteenth centuries, they are generally rectangular, up to 2 x 4m in size and usually 2 to 3m deep. They are built of two to three brick thicknesses, vaulted and nearly indestructible. Of little inherent interest and containing almost no objects of archaeological or artistic value, these tombs presented the major obstacle that was encountered. They often penetrate to the lowest level of existing structural remains, obliterating all earlier masonry. Some are partly constructed of stones robbed from the earlier surrounding walls.

All work was under the author's supervision. Only dirt and stone fill was removed and sifted. Some of the stone, mosaic and marble fragments and pottery sherds found dispersed in the fill and the lower clay levels are of limited interest and will be discussed in Appendix II. Rising stone masonry was excavated to its foundations where possible. Foundations were generally excavated to a depth of at least 2m. Mortar between stones was removed only where necessary to define the sequence of adjoining walls. The present church pavement level is taken as ± 0.00 m.

29. Botto, 1938.

30. W. Paatz, "Die gothische Kirche S. Trinita in Florenz," in *Adolf Goldschmidt zu seinem 70. Geburtstag, 15. Jan. 1933*, Berlin, 1935, pp. 113f.; *idem, Werden und Wesen der Trecentoarchitektur in Toskana*, Burg b. M., 1937, hereafter, Paatz, *Trecentoarchitektur; idem*, "Die Hauptströmungen in der florentiner Baukunst des frühen hohen Mittelalters und

ihr geschichtlicher Hintergrund," *Mitt. Kunsthist. Inst. Florenz*, VI, 1940, pp. 33f.; W. and E. Paatz, *Die Kirchen von Florenz*, V, pp. 257ff.

31. R. Baldaccini, "S. Trinita nel periodo romanico," *Rivista d'Arte*, XXVI, 1950, pp. 23f., hereafter Baldaccini, 1950; "S. Trinita nel periodo gotico," *Rivista d'Arte*, XXVII, 1951-1952, pp. 57-91.

THE CAROLINGIAN ORIGINS: TRINITA I

A legal paper notarized *foras muros florentie civitatis prope ecclesiam sancte trinitatis* in 1077 is the earliest remaining documentation of the existence of a church of Santa Trinita on what is presumably the present site.[32] Since the apparently triconch structure under the present church was first uncovered, the suggestion that it considerably antedated the eleventh century has been made repeatedly.

The discussion has been complicated by the fact that this building, which was undoubtedly converted into a hall crypt at some time, was almost invariably assumed to have been the crypt of a rather vaguely defined first church comprising the adjoining trilobe piers and the interior façade fragment (cf. pp. 21f. infra) from the very beginning. The suggested date of origin has ranged from the seventh or eighth to the eleventh centuries.[33]

Richa[34] had reported in 1755 that some "old monastery documents" referred to the church as the "Chiesa della Madonna dello Spasimo" and cautiously proposed that this title might represent an alternate, perhaps older dedication. It may, however, be nothing more than a descriptive name since the church possessed then and possesses now a late fifteenth century Flemish painting of the Madonna Addolorata which is venerated in a chapel at the far end of the southern arm.[35] In his report of 1887, the restorer Castellazzi, evidently taking up Richa's remarks, concluded that the first church on the site had been dedicated to the "Madonna dello Spasimo" and that the trefoil structure being unearthed was the crypt of this church. The tradition, reported by the Abbot Niccolini, that Santa Trinita was founded by Charlemagne around 800 coincided with this pattern.

A significant step forward was taken when Middeldorf[36] confirmed a prior tentative suggestion of Carocci[37] by noting that the structure was not originally a crypt at all, but a free-standing chapel. He suggested the possible existence of a short nave in front of the trilobed western end and dated this early building in the eleventh century. Paatz[38] generally concurred in these conclusions, but inclined to an eighth or ninth century date. He pointed as additional confirmation of Middeldorf's observation to the fact that the windows were partially overlapped by the vaults and that the consoles appear to be a later insertion (Figs. 12, 19).

As it exists today, the structure has a clear width of 11.86m (=20 *braccia fior.*). The central square measures 5.11m (8.5 *braccia*) (E-W) x 4.92m (8+ *braccia*) (N-S). The slightly stilted conches to the north and south are 3.45m (6 *braccia*) and 3.49m deep respectively. The clear east-west length from the bottom-most step of the stairs is 8.59m and the western conch has a depth of 3.29m (Pl. IV). The pavement level is 2.97m under the present church pavement. This corresponds roughly to the river level. Since Trinita I is less than 75m distant from the Arno River (Figs. 1, 2), —2.97m is the lowest level at which rising walls may be expected. The surviving walls of Trinita I rise to a height of over 2.50m. At a height of 1.71m (north and west) and 1.78m (south) over the pavement, arched splay windows, 69cm wide on the inside, 17cm on the narrow outer end pierce the 67cm thick walls. They were closed with iron grates, one of which has survived *in situ* (Fig. 21).[39] They are partially overlapped by the modern vaulting system. The western window has been enlarged and closed with cement and now serves as a niche for a fifteenth century bust of the Saviour.[40]

32. Cocchi, *Chiese*, I, pp. 167f.

33. Cf. the literature cited by Paatz V, pp. 317 n. 3 and 337 n. 109.

34. Richa, *Chiese*, III, p. 141.

35. Paatz V, p. 372 n. 282.

36. U. Middeldorf, "Berichte über die Sitzungen des Institutes, 1.-14. Sitzung 1926-1928," *Mitt. Kunsthist. Inst. Florenz*, III, Heft 3, 1929, p. 144.

37. G. Carocci, *Arte e Storia*, IV, April 19, 1885.

38. Paatz V, pp. 258, 337 n. 109.

39. The window appeared untouched in the 19th century restoration. The iron bars are badly oxidized and pitted. Apparently they underwent some seven hundred years of burial. Their exact date of origin is hard to determine. They may equally well be part of the original Trinita I or a later mediaeval installation.

40. Paatz V, p. 303; formerly part of the church treasure.

Set diagonally into the western side of the northern and southern arms are rectangular niches which penetrate the walls on a slight diagonal to a depth of about a meter. Starting 25 and 43cm over the floor level respectively, they are both 49cm wide and 110 and 115cm high. The northern niche is closed at the top by a single 68cm wide and 16cm high stone slab. The southern niche is covered by a massive triangular block 9cm wide and 35cm at its highest point, dipping 2.5cm below the niche opening on either side.

The present church (Trinita IV) is not only on an axis (25-56cm) north of the preceding buildings, but its nave widens in going from east to west. While the southern piers shift but slightly south, the northern piers move progressively further north (cf. further discussion, p. 36). As a result the eastern curve of the northern Trinita I arm is wholly inaccessible, blocked by the pier foundation. An opening in the eastern curve of the southern arm corresponding to the western niches is only partially blocked by the southern pier foundation (Pl. iv). It too was originally covered by a single stone slab lintel. It was through this opening that the "crypt" was originally discovered in the 1820's when tombs were being excavated in front of the fourth left-hand chapel of the upper church. The partially refilled shaft is still visible to a height of 2.50m from the inside of this opening. Crude retaining walls, apparently inserted during the restorations, give the remaining fragment of the original niche the appearance of having been much deeper than the 70-80cm thickness of the Trinita I wall allows. Tests made in June, 1961 proved conclusively that these walls do not bind with the Trinita I masonry. They are evidently later, probably recent insertions.

The entire eastern end of this primary structure has been affected by alterations including the steps leading down to it, the walls flanking the door and the trilobe piers behind them and particularly by the massive foundations.

The cement pavement, laid at the time of the late nineteenth century restorations, was poured over a shallow footing of river stones laid over the hard red clay soil at a level corresponding to that of the Arno banks. Excavation of the soil to a depth of about 40cm produced an abundance of unpainted and unglazed baked red clay amphora sherds. Similar finds were later made at the —3m level elsewhere in the church (cf. Appendix II).

An interesting result of these test excavations was the observation that the early building was not set on regular foundations. A test at the corner between the west and north arms revealed the wall set directly on the hard clay soil beneath. Elsewhere, e.g., at the opposite corner between the west and south arms, the wall is set on fairly solid stone foundations bound with a coarse mortar to an excavated depth of over 70cm (Fig. 19). The foundations follow the curve of the northern and southern conch walls irregularly, partly running in front of the wall, then disappearing under it.

A major question, namely the original plan of the eastern end, remains unsolved. Prior to further excavations at this end, it is best to leave the problem open. It is equally uncertain whether the building was originally vaulted or not. The massive walls suggest vaulting and the roughly 5m span of the central square is not prohibitive in this respect. It is possible to visualize apsidal domes, perhaps in conjunction with barrel vaults over the arms and a groin vault over the central square. A wooden covering need not be excluded, however, and remains the more likely possibility.

In view of the uncertainty concerning the original plan and elevation, it is hazardous to discuss the building as a type. Whatever its form, whether trefoil with or without a short nave or even quatrefoil, the conch form and the small size, whether vaulted or not, are not unusual characteristics among the small repertory of Italian and Northern buildings of the sixth to ninth centuries. Various buildings spring to mind; the nearest geographically is the trefoil chapel of Santa Maria di Castelseprio.[41] The tiny quatrefoil chapel of the Holy Cross near Hersfeld (7.34 x

41. G. P. Bognetti, G. Chierici and A. de Capitani d'Arzago, *Santa Maria di Castelseprio*, Milan, 1948. Cf. also C. R. Morey, "Castelseprio and the Byzantine Renaissance," ART BULLETIN, XXXIV, 1952, pp. 189f.

7.34m),[42] perhaps of the ninth century, and Saint Stephen in Werden on the Ruhr (819-827) are German variants and Saint-Laurent in Grenoble and the baptistery in Venasque[43] Frankish versions of the *cella trichorae* theme common in Rome and the Near East in the fourth and fifth centuries.[44]

Comparison of the rising masonry of Trinita I (cf. Appendix I) with the documented and carefully studied Carolingian masonry in Saint-Denis[45] confirms a date in that period. The masonry, surviving or excavated, belonging to Fulrad's church (775f.) is very similar: large, hewn ashlars of varying sizes; irregular or no foundations. Comparison with the surviving rising walls of Hilduin's chapel (832) in the crypt of the twelfth century Saint-Denis reveals an exact correspondence in the relative sizes of the ashlar masonry. Crosby's excavation of the 832 wall further disclosed an analogous situation regarding the foundations which vary in height with the rolling ground. "In some instances . . . the foundations are almost non-existent." We are safe, I would venture, in accepting a date between the last quarter of the eighth and the first half of the ninth century for Trinita I.

Most problematical is the question of the original function or dedication of this small building. Situated on the shore of the Arno just outside the walls of the early mediaeval town near a small postern gate whose name, the Porta Rossa, is still borne by the street leading from it, the structure seems to have been a small pilgrimage chapel. The niches in the side arms probably served as reliquaries.[46] The importance of the relic cult of Trinita I may explain its subsequent preservation and transformation. Beyond this there is only the ambiguous tradition reported by Richa.

TRINITA II—CA. 1060 TO CA. 1180

At some time after its completion, Trinita I underwent a radical transformation. A nave and two aisles, divided by columns, were built against the remaining three conches of Trinita I, 1.49m above the original level. Two trilobe piers abutting Trinita I and the interior façade of this second building were discovered during the restorations of 1885f. Since no detailed report concerning this work survives, there is no way of knowing the state in which the remains around the eastern end of Trinita I were found. However, it is possible to describe what was done at that time in the process of restoration. With the exception of the two lowest, all the steps leading down to the "crypt" level and the retaining walls flanking them are modern. The restorers left a narrow passage on both sides around the trilobe piers on the level of Trinita II (—1.48m) (Figs. 14, 22, 23). The vaults were found demolished, in the state in which they were left when the complex was destroyed. The remains of colonettes, capitals and bases as well as the consoles in the walls made it evident that previous to its destruction the room had been covered by vaults supported by sixteen colonettes (including two buried under the later pier foundations) and (originally) eighteen consoles. New colonettes with capitals meticulously copied after surviving original fragments which may still be seen lying in the "crypt" were set up and concrete vaults constructed over them. The front and back rows were given modified block capitals, the center row reduced leaf capitals. Such, more or less, must have been the appearance of the room at the time of its destruction when the pier foundations were inserted and a new church was built over it.

The point of junction between Trinita I and II is critical for the building history. While this point is blocked on the southern side by the pier foundation, it is at least partly accessible on the

42. R. Wesenberg, "S. Crucis bei Hersfeld," *Zeitschrift f. Kunstgeschichte*, XVIII, 1955, pp. 61-67.

43. Grenoble: J. Hubert, "La 'crypte' de Saint-Laurent de Grenoble," in *Arte del primo millenio*, Turin, 1953, pp. 327f. Venasque: may also be Carolingian or as late as the 10th or 11th century: cf. J. Hubert, *L'architecture religieuse du haut moyen âge en france*, Paris, 1952, s.v.

44. For a complete discussion in the light of new evidence and all recent literature: G. Forsyth, *The Church of St.* *Martin at Angers*, Princeton, 1953, p. 146 n. 256 and p. 148 n. 264. Cf. also I. Lavin, "The House of the Lord," ART BULLETIN, XLIV, 1962, pp. 1-27.

45. S. McKnight Crosby, *The Abbey of St.-Denis, 475-1122*, I, New Haven, 1942, pp. 128f., figs. 24-25.

46. Similar niches at Hexham: A. W. Clapham, *English Romanesque Architecture before the Conquest*, Oxford, 1930, p. 154. Carolingian "compound martyria": cf. the author's *Medieval Architecture*, New York, 1962, pp. 14f.

northern side and visible both from the "crypt" itself and from the narrow shaft behind the trefoil pier left by the nineteenth century excavators. On its western side, i.e., toward Trinita I, the pier extends in the form of a pilaster, originally covered by a coat of stucco fluting, a remaining fragment of which may still be seen (Fig. 15). While there is no certainty about the exact state in which the excavators found this point and what changes were made during the restoration, it would appear that this pilaster and the trefoil pier behind were always at least partially visible from the lower level. Pier and pilaster are founded on a massive wall which runs out from behind the later pier foundation for 45cm, then projects west 23cm or the width of one stone course, then the upper courses of the wall continue straight for another 1.01m, ending on a line with the southern extreme of the northern trefoil pier (wall IIa-I). The lower two courses run south at a slight angle. At the 1.01m point there is a crude indentation marking a clearly visible and roughly vertical building line (Figs. 15-18). From here the wall continues another 1.89m in a different masonry extending from floor to vaulting. The same masonry continues on the other side of the door and disappears behind the later southern pier foundation (wall IIb).

The wall on which the trefoil pier and pilaster are founded is composed of large blocks identical with the masonry of Trinita II. It seems likely that the eastern wall of Trinita I was demolished to the level of Trinita I and the trefoil pier founded directly on it. The slight shift of direction between the upper and the lower courses suggest that the upper part of the curving Trinita I wall was dismantled at this point and then reassembled to serve as a straight retaining wall under the line at which the side aisle of Trinita II adjoined the lower room.

This reconstructed eastern wall was built as regularly as possible, evidently to make it blend with the remaining Trinita I enclosing walls. At this point a first important incongruity must be noted. The crypt vaults cut directly over the stucco fluting of the exposed lower part of the pilaster (Fig. 15). The question arises: why make this pilaster with its elaborate stucco fluting at all, merely in order to have this short inorganic lower part visible from the crypt? Why not simply close all but a central stairway off against Trinita I with a solid wall?

There is another piece of evidence: a fragment of curved steps crudely imposed on the northern trefoil (Fig. 22). A modern retaining wall runs over it, marking the apparent limit of the 1885f. excavation.

It would seem that we are dealing with two wholly separate building phases in Trinita II, different in time, structure and function. These phases may be labeled Trinita IIa and IIb and are best discussed in that order.

MARTYRIUM CHURCH: TRINITA IIa—CA. 1060

The features we have examined suggest that in the Trinita IIa period, the attached Trinita I was not turned into a crypt at all. The new nave and aisles were a large basilical room, built against the eastern end of the now partially truncated Trinita I. The lower church remained at its full height, while the trilobe piers with the pilasters facing the open end of Trinita I framed a broad access from the upper church. Since the wall IIb on either side of the present narrow access steps serves primarily as a support for the later vaulting, it need not be considered a part of Trinita IIa. One might rather expect a broad set of steps leading down from the level of Trinita II and opening in its full width into Trinita I.[47] This hypothesis was confirmed when the pavement of the lower structure was lifted in September 1957.

Wall IIa under the pilaster was found to rest directly on a shallow (41cm high) footing of loose rubble laid without mortar binding on the hard clay soil beneath (Fig. 17). The fact that this footing begins directly under the line of the nineteenth century pavement indicates that this

47. Cf. Paatz's similar suggestion (v, p. 265) for a reconstruction of the stairs leading down to Trinita I *after* its conversion into a crypt.

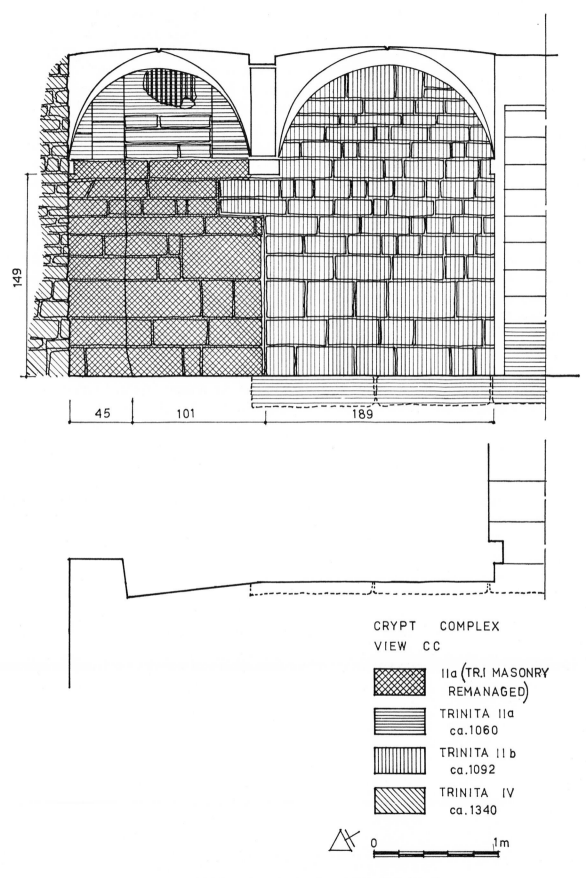

1. Santa Trinita, "Crypt," elevation of East Wall (detail)
with northern Trinita II trefoil pier

line corresponds to that of the original pavement, a conclusion also warranted by the tests at other points in Trinita I. Previous to the repaving, a stone step was visible imbedded in the pavement between the jambs of the door at the foot of the stairs (Fig. 15). When the pavement was lifted, this step was found to extend to either side under wall IIb. It is composed of roughly 1m long and 20cm high slabs founded upon another set of slabs below them. They disappear behind the later pier foundation on the southern side, but end just to the north of the dividing line between walls IIa and IIb (Fig. 18). This step is clearly part of an original set of stairs leading down the width of the nave from the Trinita II level. Wall IIb was built over this step in the subsequent conversion, while the jambs of the central doorway are built over the first rising step which also appears to be original (Fig. 14). As we have already observed, all other steps in the present stairway are modern. It is difficult to judge in what condition the excavators found these steps. The modern cement floor of the passageways flanking the stairs at the level of Trinita II and the modern retaining walls around the piers have hidden what evidence might remain there.[48]

Another question: precisely how was the side aisle of Trinita IIa closed off against the curving walls of the lower church? Our excavations of February-March, 1958 clarified this problem in nearly every respect. The steps imposed on the base of the trefoil pier and visible in the northern shaft left by the earlier excavators, break off over the third step. In the space directly behind them to the right of the trilobe pier and in front of the rising masonry of the later massive pier foundation, buried under loose dirt, a wall abutting the northern lobe of the trefoil pier and consisting of a single thickness of ashlars came to light (Fig. 26). Its regular *pietra forte* masonry corresponds to that of the façade visible on the interior of the present façade. Excavations in the northern side aisle of the present church in front of the fourth right-hand chapel (Bartolini-Salimbeni) (Pl. VI, Figs. 24, 25, 27-32) revealed that this wall continues to a point over a meter beyond the outer extreme of the northern arm of Trinita I. Hence the side wall of Trinita II was *not* flush with the width of Trinita I as earlier authors[49] had supposed and the Trinita II side aisle was considerably more than one-half the width of its nave. The trefoil pier and the abutting side-aisle end wall suggest the existence of an engaged quarter column in the corner of the side aisle carrying a blind arch or entablature. No trace of the corner, an engaged column or the Trinita II side wall was found during our excavations. The reasons for this will become apparent in a more detailed examination of the side-aisle excavation in the following section.

The search for the side wall of Trinita II elsewhere remained without success. Test excavations in front of the second southern side chapel and the southern portal undertaken in October 1957 (Pl. II, A, K) encountered the same obstacles found elsewhere in the church, namely later tombs. It was unfeasible to dismantle these almost indestructible hindrances. Tests across the width of the side aisle failed to reveal any traces of previous foundations.

Another test made at that time in front of the southern portal produced no trace of the aisle wall. The dislocated fragments of a portal (possibly from Trinita II) were found incorporated in a tomb extending partly under the façade (Pl. II, Fig. 33). Also found in this tomb was the fragment of a composition pavement at level —1.63m. The fragment covers only about half of the tomb. It is crudely broken off towards the façade. The mixed brick and robbed ashlar masonry of the tomb extends down yet another .36m in the part nearest and under the façade. It was not possible to confirm positively whether the pavement extended outside of the tomb. Its level and composition suggest that it may be a part of the Trinita IIa composition pavement found at —1.48m in excavation C (cf. pp. 15f. infra).

On the other hand, the remains of a building contemporary with Trinita II and rising from the —1.50m level on rubble foundations on a line 60cm in front of the first three northern side

48. It is unfeasible to demolish the cement floor and the modern steps and retaining walls and unlikely that such excavations would turn up significant evidence. Excavations in the nave further to the east and to either side of the steps, however, might settle the problem of a possible "Trinita I nave."

49. Cf. Paatz V, p. 266; also Baldaccini, 1950, pp. 23f.

chapels (excavation D), suggests that the extreme northern limit of the Trinita II aisle end wall found at C is roughly identical with the original line of the Trinita II side wall since this would leave just about one meter between it and the adjoining building on the north (Pls. III, VII, Figs. 25, 35, 36). The remains of this adjoining structure will be discussed below (*casa solariata* wall).

Trinita IIa with the remaining part of Trinita I attached to its western end and accessible by a broad set of steps running down between two trefoil piers (text fig. 2) is an unusual phenomenon

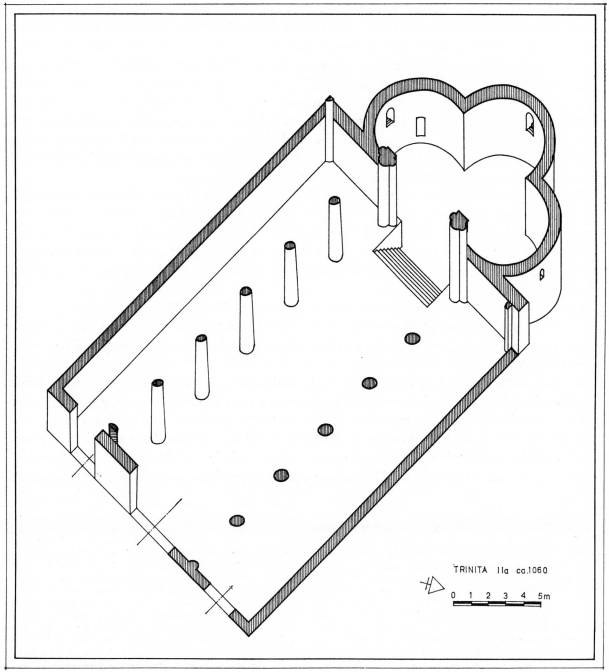

2. Reconstruction of Trinita IIa

in Florentine mediaeval architecture, though it has a parallel in another peculiar eleventh century complex, San Pier Scheraggio.[50] Its possible significance and date can only be surmised from a combination of inherent and historical factors. A church of Santa Trinita in Florence is documented

50. H. Saalman, "Florence: Santa Trinita I and II and the 'Crypts' under Santa Reparata and San Pier Scheraggio," *J.* *Soc. Arch. Historians*, XXI, 1962, pp. 179-187.

for the first time in 1077. The Vallombrosians, however, did not take possession of the site until 1092.[51] Hence, there is no reason to assume that the church existing prior to 1092 was in any way connected with or suitable for the monastic cult.

The 1077 document does not in itself provide a *terminus ante quem* for Trinita IIa since it might refer to Trinita I as well.[52] A hypothetical date for the construction of Trinita IIa rests largely on the comparative chronology for eleventh century Florentine churches based on masonry studies established by Walter Horn.[53]

Comparison of Trinita IIa masonry (Figs. 9, 25, 26) with the masonry of Santi Apostoli (before 1075; Horn: 1059-1075) and particularly with San Pier Scheraggio (dedicated 1068) reveals a very close relationship. The masonry is characterized by even courses of smooth rectangular ashlars, rarely exceeding 15cm in height and averaging 20 to 40cm in length. As Horn has noted, occasional and unsystematical instances of an alternation between thick and thin courses may be noticed in these buildings. This is in contrast to the regular alternation of courses that marks masonry datable in the later eleventh and early twelfth century (San Giovanni, attic; San Miniato, upper zone of apse and clerestory. It should be observed, however, that the lower masonry zone in Trinita II, Santi Apostoli and San Pier Scheraggio is marked by an almost complete absence of thin courses and by no alternation of courses whatever.

This characteristic brings these buildings into parallel with San Miniato where the very regular courses in the lower parts of the rising masonry also consist largely of high and short, often nearly square ashlar blocks (cf. particularly Trinita IIa) (Fig. 9). Contrary to Horn and Paatz, these courses are not confined to the eastern (apse) wall of San Miniato, but extend around as much of the building as is accessible to view.[54] The arched splay windows of Trinita IIa and Santi Apostoli are nearly identical.

The consoles bearing the blind arches over the recess in the Trinita IIa façade wall (Fig. 9) and the arches themselves find their counterparts bearing the vaulting in the eastern side of the so-called crypt under San Pier Scheraggio which we attribute to the eleventh century building period of that church.[55]

We may, consequently, join Horn and Paatz in attributing a date of about 1060-1070 to Trinita IIa. This date, furthermore, is far enough in advance of 1092 to allow for an arrangement which had to be completely altered to meet the needs of the monks, probably shortly after 1092.

Trinita IIa was created, not to supplant the earlier building, but to make it accessible to greater numbers of the faithful when, at a time of renewed church building in Florence, the tiny chapel had become inadequate. The need for additional space and the problems posed by the periodic inunda-

51. Cf. notes 12-13 supra.

52. Paatz V, p. 318 n. 5.

53. W. Horn, "Das Florentiner Baptisterium," *Mitt. Kunsthist. Inst. Florenz*, v, 1938, pp. 100-151; *idem*, "Romanesque Churches in Florence and Their Chronology and Stylistic Development," ART BULLETIN, XXV, 1943, pp. 112f.

54. Basing themselves on prior observations by Ulrich Middeldorf, Horn (1943) and Paatz (IV, pp. 211f.) have stated the view that the eastern wall of the crypt of San Miniato is to be dated 1014 and identified with the *confessio* planned by Bishop Hildebrand in that year. They agree, however, that the entire remainder of the church was built sometime after 1060-1070. K. J. Conant's dates, 1018-1062 (*Carolingian and Romanesque Architecture, 800 to 1200*, Baltimore, 1959, p. 231) are based on E. W. Anthony's outdated study of 1927 (*Early Florentine Architecture and Decoration*, Cambridge, Mass., 1927, pp. 21f.). Horn's and Paatz's conclusions are founded largely on the observation that the lower stone courses of the apse wall differ from the upper parts. The lower section consists of large, irregular ashlar courses while the upper zone is laid in regularly alternating courses of thin and thick blocks. This situation prevails, however, not only along the apse wall. The identical large block masonry can be fol-

lowed along the southern crypt wall (accessible from an adjoining cellar under the 14th century sacristy, Fig. 72). Although repeated collapses of the campanile have led to restorations in the eastern parts of the northern side wall, the large block masonry of the apse wall can be followed west on this side as far as the Portugal Chapel with certainty. Recent (1964) removal of the modern marble revetments along the interior aisle walls of San Miniato confirms this observation (Fig. 73). The indication is not that the lower masonry represents an earlier building period, but that the masonry technique varied depending on the height reached. The choice is between dating *all* of the church either 1014 or in the last quarter of the century (so already Luigi Dami, "La basilica di S. Miniato al Monte," *Bollettino d'Arte*, 1915, p. 219). Horn's other observations make the latter alternative preferable. Bishop Hildebrand's *confessio* may have been an annular crypt with *confessio* built under the hypothetical apse of the preceding (early Christian?) church, or a small chapel attached to the earlier building. It might even have been a separate chamber *under* it (*vide* San Pier Scheraggio, note 50 supra).

55. Cf. note 50 supra.

tions[56] were resolved by the Trinita II annex. The curious combination of the trefoil chapel and basilical nave recalls early Christian *martyrium* complexes in the Near East and Italy dating from the fourth to the sixth centuries.[57]

The location of the main altar of Trinita IIa may be supposed to have been in its hypothetical fifth nave bay (text fig. 2),[58] visible to the congregation, but allowing free access to Trinita I behind. A related arrangement still exists at San Miniato al Monte.[59]

CRYPT, CHOIR AND THE VALLOMBROSIANS: TRINITA IIb—1092f.

When the monks of the Benedictine reform order founded at Vallombrosa by St. Giovanni Gualberto in 1039 took possession of Santa Trinita in 1092, profound changes in the structure and function of the existing building seem to have become necessary. It appears reasonable to connect the creation of the hall crypt within the confines of the original Trinita I walls and of a monks' choir and presbytery above its vaults with this event. This supposition is supported not only by the late eleventh century character of the surviving colonette capital fragments in the crypt (Fig. 21),[60] but also by the fact that the evident prototype for the crypt and choir idea, San Miniato, was being built in these very years.[61]

The exact nature of the alterations made at this time was revealed by excavations in the fourth bay of the northern side aisle of the present church (Pl. v, Figs. 24, 25, 27-32).

As we have noted, the end wall of the Trinita IIa side aisle, abutting the right-hand trefoil pier in front of Trinita I, could be followed for over 2m into the side aisle of the present church. At its highest point, the end wall IIa is preserved up to a level .70m under the present pavement (level ±0.00). No trace of the side-aisle corner or any part of the northern Trinita II side wall was found. Instead, the wall continues irregularly up to the chapel steps in crude work, clearly not rising masonry. We shall return to the possible significance of this continuation in our discussion of Trinita III (infra, p. 27).

At level —1.48, the level of Trinita II corresponding to the base of the trefoil piers, the composition pavement of this church appeared (Fig. 28); pavement traces were also found on the southern side of the building (cf. pp. 12f. supra). Directly over this pavement and built against the end wall IIa, the fragmentary remains of a circular step with a calculated radius of 2.25m, and a smaller concentric step above it, came to light. The depth of the steps is 30cm, the riser is 20cm. The arcs of the two steps coincide precisely with the arcs of the two bottom steps imposed on the

56. In its position on the flat banks of the Arno, barely above the water level, Trinita I must have been periodically under water. Thus the decision to raise the surrounding level and build the new addition 1.49m above the earlier level can be explained in terms of physical necessity. It parallels a pattern characteristic of what may be called "river-bank churches," both in Florence (San Pier Scheraggio, San Jacopo in Ripa d'Arno, San Niccolo Oltrarno) and elsewhere along the river, all of which were rebuilt at consecutively higher levels. San Michele in Borgo, Pisa (M. Salmi, *L'architettura romanica in Toscana*, Milan-Rome, 1927, p. 41, hereafter, Salmi) was partly rebuilt, but not raised. The crypt is now permanently under water and inaccessible. Previous to the building of the present high 19th century embankments in Florence, the areas near the river were regularly under water. In 1833 the water-line at the Pazzi Chapel was nearly 3m above ground level.

57. For a brief discussion of the combination of trefoil apse and basilica cf. K. A. C. Creswell, *A Short Account of Early Muslim Architecture*, Baltimore, 1958, pp. 144f. See also I. Lavin, "The House of the Lord."

58. This reconstruction of Trinita II is based on the following considerations: the distance from the façade to the trefoil pier in front of Trinita I is just 22m or 36.6 *br. fior.* This

may be divided into six bays of 6 *braccia* each from axis to axis as in nearby Santi Apostoli.

59. The altar of the cross of San Giovanni Gualberto is in a similar position in front of the steps leading to the crypt of San Miniato. Middeldorf (cf. Paatz IV, pp. 232f., 278 n. 135) has dated the Romanesque parts of the altar contained in the early Renaissance ciborium (1448) in the 12th century. An altar must have existed on this spot in 1207 when the *opus sectile* pavement strip leading from the main portal to the altar was laid (Paatz IV, p. 226; Saalman, *Medieval Architecture*, pl. 71).

60. The block capitals of the crypt are almost identical with some of the capitals in the crypt under Santa Maria dell' Impruneta, dedicated in 1066 (F. Rossi, "La basilica di S. Maria dell'Impruneta," *Boll. d'Arte*, XXXV, 1950, p. 85; *idem*, "La crypta dell'Impruneta," *Palladio*, N.S., VIII, 1958, pp. 88f.).

61. The 12th century nave attached to the lower 6th century church of San Lorenzo fuori le mura, Rome, which was then similarly converted into crypt and choir, is an instance of an identical process of growth (cf. R. Krautheimer et al., *Corpus basilicarum Christianarum Romae*, II, 1, Vatican City, 1959, pp. 1f.).

northern trefoil pier, indicating that originally a semicircular stairway led from the northern side aisle of Trinita II to the choir over the crypt vaults supported by the newly inserted crypt colonettes. Six concentric steps, the smallest with a calculated diameter of 90cm, led up to the level of the choir, 1.20m above Trinita II, corresponding to the top level of the (modern cement) crypt vaults, 28cm under the present pavement.

Built against the end wall IIa on its western side and closing the spandrel between this wall and the curving wall of Trinita I, a second wall of double ashlar thickness appeared just 36cm under the present pavement. The wall runs on an east-west axis 1.15m north of the Trinita IV pier (Figs. 24, 30-32). At —1.46m, the Trinita II level, this wall projects 5-10cm. Below this level it continues down to below —3.00m. The spandrel void between the end wall IIa and the curving wall of Trinita I is filled with a loosely packed stone and mortar mix retained by the relatively thin east-west wall. At the —2.30m level of the dig at this point, one large stone was removed from this wall. While the fill is fairly solid at the top, it is packed loosely below so that hollow spaces were visible.

Part of a terra-cotta rainwater pipe consisting of conical sections with an inner upper diameter of 18cm narrowing at the bottom and fitted into the section below appeared in the corner between the east-west wall and the IIa end wall. The tube ran down to 5cm under the —1.46 level projection and then ended curving off to the north (Figs. 30, 31).

The Trinita II composition pavement is abruptly sliced off on an east-west line running just under the bottommost step of the circular stairs. The entire area on the eastern side of the Trinita IIa end wall between the circular stairs and the line of the present chapel steps on the north is filled with graves at various levels and of different periods. In the extreme northeast corner of the excavation (visible on the right in Fig. 29), a large (roughly 2 x 1m) brick grave, probably of the seventeenth or eighteenth century,[62] extends from just under the pavement level to about —1.55m. At level —1.40, just to the west of the brick tomb, appeared what may be an accidental grouping of stones in the shape of part of a horseshoe. Its significance, if any, is unclear. Extending directly under it from a point 45cm to the north of the circular steps at level —1.50 is a narrow rectangular tomb 70cm wide, enclosed within crude stone walls to a stone slab platform at a depth of —3.05m and extending northward to an unexcavated point under the "horseshoe" fragment above it. The grave contained an abundance of well-preserved skeletal fragments and traces of decomposed wood down to its lowest level. Directly adjoining this grave on its eastern side were surface traces of a second similar grave which, being directly under the brick tomb above, was left unexcavated.

The fact that these graves lie partially outside of the probable area of the Trinita II side aisle and that the composition pavement which originally would have covered the entire Trinita II side aisle has been removed, provides a probable *terminus post quem* for the graves. Since they are fully contained within the side aisle of the succeeding church (cf. infra, pp. 27f.), they may be dated any time after the demolition of Trinita II, but evidently before the creation of the brick tomb above. The composition of the stone graves also provides a possible explanation for the total disappearance of the northern Trinita II side wall in the portion investigated. When these graves were dug, as noted to a depth of over 3m, all then-remaining traces of the Trinita II side wall and its foundation were removed. The possible hypothesis (suggested by its crude continuation) that the Trinita II side wall ran as far north as the line of the chapel steps, was negated by the discovery of the *casa solariata* wall in front of the first three chapels next to the façade (cf. infra, pp. 18f.). The material used in the creation of the stone retaining walls of these graves consists entirely of irregular ashlar masonry probably robbed from the Trinita II side walls.

Just to the west of the IIa end wall, in front of the chapel steps to the north of the east-west

---

62. A similar grave nearby contained the remains of two copper crosses datable in the 17th century (cf. Appendix II).

trench dug to level —3.00 in front of the IIb spandrel retaining wall, followed yet another series of late brick tombs which were left uninvestigated.

It is possible to reconstruct Trinita IIb in nearly every significant detail (text fig. 3). The Trinita IIa nave was left unaltered. The broad flight of eight steps leading down to the Trinita I

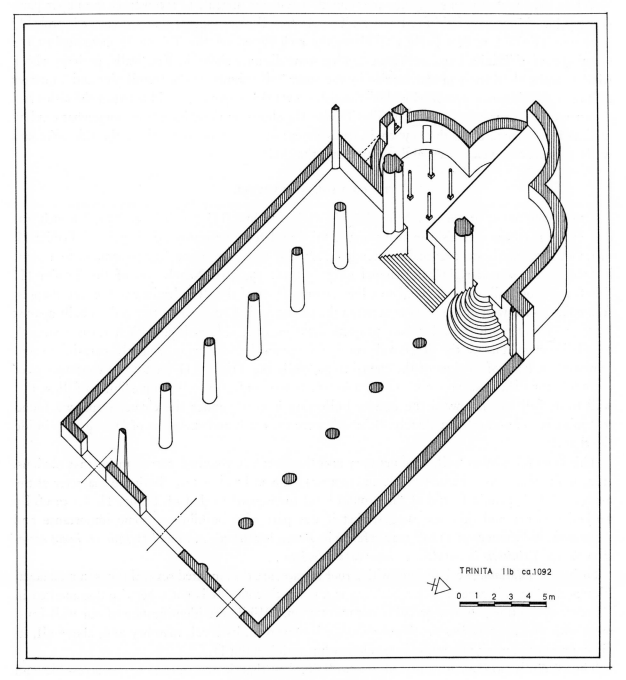

3. Reconstruction of Trinita IIb

level from the line of the trefoil piers was blocked on the second step above the lower level by the new IIb wall which carried the groin vaults of the eastern bays of the newly inserted hall crypt on console brackets. The stone and mortar fill in the northern spandrel void between Trinita I and IIa and the new IIb retaining wall (we may assume a similar arrangement on the southern side which could not be explored in this campaign), suggest that the choir area was extended outward over the filled-in space and closed off by the outer retaining-enclosing wall. The part of the Trinita II side-aisle end wall directly in front of the enlarged choir area must have been demolished to the level of the choir while the semicircular steps, to the right of and partly (and rather crudely) imposed on the base of the northern trefoil pier, now gave onto the choir over the newly filled-in spandrel platform within the outer limits marked by the IIb retaining-closing wall.

While the essential points are thus ascertained, it remains difficult to reconstruct the upper parts at the point of junction of Trinita I and II. The IIa trefoil piers suggest that a great arch probably gave into Trinita I while a gable wall above the arch closed off the Trinita II nave against the abutting roof of Trinita I and perhaps extended some distance above it. End walls, perhaps with a window and a blind framing arch carried by the outer half column of the trefoil pier and a quarter column in the side-aisle corner, closed off the aisles toward the spandrel void between the aisles and the curving side conches of Trinita I. The Trinita IIa elevation must have been somewhat crudely modified in order to effect the new choir arrangement by removing as much of the side-aisle end walls as obstructed a clear view and entrance into the choir.

THE CASA SOLARIATA WALL

During the course of our search for the side wall of Trinita III (cf. infra p. 27), a trench was dug in the northern side aisle in front of the third and fourth right-hand chapels of Trinita IV (Pl. VI). The trench was eventually extended, partly by tunneling under the pavement, to a point in front of the second right-hand chapel (Figs. 34-36, 39, 40). Nearly 5m of the Trinita III side-foundation wall was uncovered on a line 34cm in front of the steps leading to the side chapels. At a point 1.52m west of the pilaster between the second and third chapels, this wall is built against another, obviously older wall, which projects .89m into the side aisle and then turns a smooth rounded corner. Thence the older wall continues eastward, .60m wide, roughly parallel to and somewhat in front of the line of the chapel steps, while the Trinita III foundation continues over it crudely for a short distance and then breaks off. It was, unfortunately, impossible to follow this wall to its full extent toward the façade. Following it north under the chapel steps, we found that it breaks off almost immediately. Behind it were the earth and skeletons of later graves inside the chapel.

This is no foundation wall. The masonry and the carefully rounded corner make that obvious. Its actual foundations (of crude rubble and mortar) begin at level —1.50. Both the character of the masonry (cf. Appendix I) and of the ground level correspond to that of Trinita II. Its carefully worked masonry and thickness suggest that it was part of a building of some importance and dimension. A document of 1124[63] may refer to it: *Breve investionis . . . quod factum est iuxta ecclesiam Sancte Trinitatis in eiusdem ecclesie casa solariata . . .*

Such *casae solariatae*, i.e. buildings with a roof terrace, are documented several times in mediaeval Florence.[64] The existence of such a building in a monastic complex is not otherwise documented in Florence at this time, but was probably not uncommon.[65] While the identification of our wall fragment with the *casa solariata . . . iuxta ecclesiam* is unproven, its level, masonry and, above all, its direct proximity, put it into immediate relationship with Trinita II.

The carefully worked masonry of the wall implies that it was meant to be accessible and visible from the south. Therefore we may suggest that there must have been a space of at least 1m intervening between the two structures. This is an additional reason for assuming the existence of the Trinita II side wall roughly 2m in front of the chapel steps.

63. R. Davidsohn, *Geschichte von Florenz*, I, p. 731 n. 1; cf. also R. Piattoli, ed., . . . *Le carte . . . della Cattedrale di Firenze . . .* , pp. 408f., doc. 169.

64. R. Davidsohn, *op.cit.*, p. 731 n. 1.

65. The Dominican Constitutions of 1228 indicate that the *solarium* is a regular part of the monastic buildings: *De edi-* *ficiis. Mediocres domos et humiles habeant fratres nostri, ita quod murus domorum sine solario non excedant in altitudine mensuram XII pedum, et cum solario XX . . .* (H. Denifle, "Die Constitutionen des Predigerordens vom Jahre 1228," *Archiv für Litteratur- und Kirchengeschichte des Mittelalters*, I, 1885, p. 225.

THE MISSING LINK: TRINITA III—CA. 1175f.

The problem of the origin and date of the present church has always excited more interest than have the earlier buildings. Central to this interest has been Vasari's attribution of the church to Nicola Pisano, implying a date around the middle of the thirteenth century. Various solutions to this puzzle have been suggested. For example: 1) the church is by Nicola Pisano, or at least begun by him, hence ca. 1250; Vasari is right; 2) the church was begun ca. 1250, but not by Pisano; Vasari is partially right; 3) the church is later (fourteenth century); there never was a mid-thirteenth century project, hence no basis for Vasari's attribution whatever; 4) the present church was built in the fourteenth century, but there *was* a building of ca. 1250, perhaps by Pisano; Vasari is wrong, but there is some basis for his attribution.

Limburger[66] endorsed the third hypothesis, rejected Vasari's attribution and considered the building a product of the fourteenth century. Other earlier authors who referred to the problem did not enter into a detailed discussion.[67] More recently Walter Paatz[68] has advocated the first alternative with allowance for the possibility of the second. He suggested two building periods: the first from ca. 1251-1258 to about 1280 (eastern part of nave); the second (based on documents published by Botto[69]) from 1362 to about 1405 (western part of nave and transept).

Fasola[70] agreed with Paatz. Krönig[71] raised some objections, particularly to the Pisano attribution, but left the major thesis intact. Keller[72] returned to Limburger's position, but felt that the present church is somehow "tied to a Dugento groundplan." Baldaccini[73] moved the entire present church with the exception of the first four side chapels on either side back to 1251-1289.

While these hypotheses consider the present building as the third in a series preceded by Trinita I and II, new documentary evidence led Carlo Botto[74] to yet another possibility within the Vasari framework. He postulated a third church (Trinita III), begun about 1250, perhaps by Pisano, and completed by 1327, but almost wholly demolished when the present church (Trinita IV) was built after 1362.

A reexamination of the Trinita problem must be based on consideration of some fundamental facts. In summary: a) there is a difference of 1.48m in level between Trinita II and the present church and b) a difference of about 4m in width between these buildings; c) there is a slight shift of axis between the preceding buildings and the present church, measurable as 25cm at the façade and 56cm at the entrance to the "crypt";[75] d) the first four southern chapels are shallower in plan than the other chapels around the church; they contain frescoes generally dated before the middle

66. W. Limburger, *Die Gebäude von Florenz*, Leipzig, 1910, No. 694, p. 170.

67. K. Frey, *Die Loggia del Lanzi zu Florenz*, Berlin, 1885, pp. 24, 86; idem, "Arnolfo di Cambio," in Thieme-Becker, *Allgemeines Lexikon der bildenden Künstler*, II, Leipzig, 1908, p. 143; idem (ed.), G. Vasari, *Le vite . . . ,* I, pp. 575, 824. Frey expressed an early doubt whether Nicola Pisano was an architect at all (*Loggia dei Lanzi*, p. 86), but mainly in order to attribute Santa Trinita to Arnolfo, an opinion he later revised; C. Enlart, *Les origines françaises de l'architecture gothique en Italie*, Paris, 1894, p. 161; G. Dehio and G. v. Bezold, *Die kirchliche Baukunst des Abendlandes*, Stuttgart, 1901, II, p. 511; A. Nardini Despotti Mospignotti, *Il Duomo di San Giovanni*, Florence, 1902, p. 139 n. 2; I. B. Supino, *Gli albori del arte fiorentina*, Florence, 1906, p. 132; Cocchi, *Chiese*, pp. 167f.; Salmi, p. 34; E. W. Anthony, *Early Florentine Architecture and Decoration*, p. 43.

68. A brief statement of Paatz's early ideas: "Die Gothische Kirche S. Trinita in Florenz," in *Adolf Goldschmidt zu seinem 70. Geburtstag, 15. Jan. 1933*, pp. 113f.; idem, *Trecentoarchitektur*, pp. 23f. Paatz's conclusions appear to be based partly on earlier studies by M. Wackernagel, "Zur älteren Baugeschichte von S. Maria Novella," *Mitt. Kunsthist. Inst.*

Florenz, III, 1931, p. 353 n. 2. Final summary: Paatz V, pp. 257f.

69. Cf. infra.

70. G. Nicco Fasola, "Induzioni su Nicola Pisano Architetto," *L'Arte*, N.S., IX, 1938, pp. 315f.; idem, *Nicola Pisano*, Rome, 1941, pp. 175f. See also P. Metz's cautious comments "Die florentiner Domfassade des Arnolfo di Cambio," *Jahrbuch der preuss. Kunstsammlungen*, LVIII, 1938, p. 156 n. 1.

71. W. Krönig, Review of W. Paatz, *Trecentoarchitektur*, *Zeitschrift f. Kunstgesch.*, VIII, 1939, pp. 203f.; idem, "Toskana und Apulien, Beiträge zum Problemkreis der Herkunft des Nicola Pisano," *Zeitschr. f. Kunstgesch.*, XVI, 1953, pp. 101f.

72. H. Keller, *Giovanni Pisano*, Vienna, 1942, p. 12 n. 3.

73. Baldaccini, 1951-1952, pp. 57-91; cf. also Baldaccini, 1950, pp. 23f. A. Parronchi's essay involving Santa Trinita ("Architettura visualizzata," in *Studi su la 'dolce' Prospettiva*, Milan, 1964, pp. 91ff., particularly pp. 97-104) was evidently written without knowledge of our work, although he cites the résumé of this dissertation in *Marsyas*, X, 1961, p. 7.

74. Botto, 1938, pp. 1f.

75. This variation is due to a slight shift of direction.

of the fourteenth century and differ among themselves in details[76] suggesting that they are not part of a unified plan but were individually erected; since a window faces out from the third to the fourth chapel, that chapel *must* be later than the third.[77]

There are, in addition, the archival documents, published by Botto, which ascertain that all parts of the present church except the first four southern chapels were built *after* 1362.[78]

Several questions require consideration: 1) Has it ever been established that there *was* a mid-thirteenth century project for rebuilding Santa Trinita? 2) If so, does that reconstruction concern the existing church? 3) What is the relation of the façade in the Ghirlandaio fresco (Fig. 2) to the successive buildings on the site and to the interior façade visible since the restoration? 4) What about the left-hand chapels? Differing among themselves, and apparently built at various times *before* work on most of the present church was begun, are they part of a coherent church project? They *cannot* form part of Trinita II whose level was 1.48m lower. 5) Is there, finally, a solution to this problem which is not in contrast with the given factors on which this discussion is based?

A MID-THIRTEENTH CENTURY PROJECT?

None of the documents before the mid-fourteenth century refer to actual construction or to the beginning or completion of any such work, though they attest the existence of one of the succeeding churches of Santa Trinita at the time of writing. All of the various dates ranging from 1178 (*jus parrocchiale*) to 1258 (façade tondo),[79] therefore, merit consideration on an equal basis and any of them may or may not imply the beginning or completion of a new (post-Trinita II) church. Let us consider the date on the plaque here since it is basic to the assumption of a mid-thirteenth century project and the Nicola Pisano tradition.

Richa[80] linked the plaque "come un'ostia" over the church portal with the monogrammatic date 1257 (or 1258) to a tradition that the Guelfs and Ghibellines had entered the church in the course of factional fighting and had been expelled by the display of the sacred host in this year. Paatz[81] dismissed this story as a later invention created to explain the plaque. He felt that it marked the foundation date of Nicola Pisano's church.

But the few later thirteenth century dates we have are difficult to reconcile with a new church project. Why, e.g., should Cimabue have been commissioned to paint his huge Madonna about 1285 for a church which remained an unfinished fragment eighty years later? Where in the small Romanesque building, encumbered with the apparatus of a new church in construction at a new higher level would the documented war councils of 1289 and 1301 have taken place? These considerations signified to Botto and Baldaccini that their respective 1250f. churches must have been largely finished about 1285-1289. But they contradict the likelihood of Paatz's theory.

76. Paatz V, pp. 273, 344 n. 147; Baldaccini (1951-1952, p. 59 n. 6) made an important observation before the outer wall of the first three left-hand chapels, damaged by the explosion of the Ponte Santa Trinita in 1944, was repaired and covered with a heavy plaster coating in restorations of 1956. He reports the following: "Nel punto dove c'è un contrafforte che delimita la prima dalla seconda cappella, in seguito all' esplosione che distrusse il ponte S. Trinita, si vede uno stacco netto per tutta l'altezza del contrafforte comprovante, per il pietrame non incastrato in continuità, che la seconda cappelle [sic] fu appoggiata in un tempo successivo." He also noted that the first chapel had no window while the windows of the second and third chapels were at different heights and had different profiles (so also Paatz). Mons. Bucetti, the former prior of Santa Trinita, informed me that the explosion of Ponte Santa Trinita had nothing to do with damage to the church. This is supported by the fact that the Palazzo Gianfigliazzi, between the bridge and the church, was almost untouched. Don Bucetti claimed that German occupation troops set off a mine under the altar of the Strozzi Chapel in order to enter

a textile establishment, then directly adjoining. Cf. also F. Hartt, *Florentine Art under Fire*, Princeton, 1949, p. 126.

77. When building was begun on the northern chapels after 1362, a document, dated Jan. 3, 1364 st.c. (Arch. di. St., Firenze, *Conv.* 224, Fa. 222. c. 237) refers to the third southern chapel as already in existence: . . . *executores testamenti Ser Cialli . . . volentes edificare et edificari facere unam cappellam in Ecclesie Ste Trinitatis predicte ad honorem Dei et Beati Luce Evangeliste iuxta dispositionem dicti Ser Cialli, designaverunt locum ubi cadit tertia ex cappellis que noviter hedificantur in dicta Ecclesia et qui locus et que Cappella est et erit opposito Cappelle Sancte Caterine existentis in dicta Ecclesia ex altero latere dicte ecclesie, et parietes posteriores fundatas et parte extra fundumenta muratas esse . . .* The wording indicates a finished church, i.e. Trinita III, not Paatz's three- or four-bay fragment.

78. Botto, 1938, pp. 1f.

79. Cf. p. 3 supra.

80. Richa, *Chiese*, III, p. 143.

81. Paatz V, p. 321 n. 15.

Whatever the precise significance of the round marble tondo with the inscription 1257 (or 1258) on the former façade of the church, it may provide a clue to the origin of Vasari's date and attribution. Is it hard to suppose that the biographer, standing in front of a church reportedly dear to Michelangelo,[82] seeing this plaque (then *in situ*), connected the date with an event famous in Florentine history and with a famous artist and made an architect out of Nicola Pisano?[83] It should be emphasized that *no* source prior to Vasari, particularly Giovanni Villani, who was closer to the events and might have known, ever mentioned the name Nicola Pisano in connection with Santa Trinita.

THE FRESCO AND THE INTERIOR FAÇADE

Both the pre-Buontalenti façade (demolished after 1592), shown in Domenico Ghirlandaio's fresco of 1479-1486 in the Sassetti Chapel in Santa Trinita (Fig. 2), and the vestiges of the old interior façade, visible since the 1880's (Fig. 9), are crucial to this discussion.

Some authors have been struck by seemingly strange aspects of the fresco façade. Karl Frey, who dated the façade and the present church in the fourteenth century, saw what appeared to be arches or niches over the central door.[84] Study of the fresco suggests that these elements are not "over," but actually *part* of the portal itself, i.e., the panels of a large, probably wooden, *portone*. A small hinged door, corresponding to a little over a man's height (as apparent from the fresco) is cut into this *portone*, a ubiquitous feature of Italian churches and palaces[85] and precisely the sort of genre detail Ghirlandaio would not have omitted. The doors leading into the aisles were of approximately the same size. Once this is recognized, the proportional relationship of men and doors in the fresco becomes understandable and Ghirlandaio's "trustworthiness" more likely.[86]

Flanking the upper part of the central portal, an arcade with four arches to either side, screening a shallow sham gallery in the Pisano-Luccan manner, extends to the outer extremes of the side aisles of the church, i.e., up to a pilaster strip marking the line between the side aisle and the adjoining side chapel depicted in the fresco (text fig. 4).[87] Directly over the portal, two tiers of arcades span the apparent nave width between pilaster strips that rise up above the arcades to flank a large oculus. The uppermost part of the façade is cut off by the frame of the fresco. Slim pointed windows appear in the center axes of the side aisles over the lowest row of arches. The side-aisle roof line abuts the nave wall at a level roughly equivalent to the upper limit of the oculus circumference.

While most of these features have disappeared behind the cover of the Buontalenti façade, some elements in the fresco are still *in situ* and visible, and may serve as fixed points of reference in a reconstruction as well as corroboration for Ghirlandaio's almost photographic accuracy. Directly behind the southern jamb of the Buontalenti portal, a fragment of the older portal visible in the fresco remains in place (Figs. 8, 44). The buttress-like jamb with a piece of the segmental-arched lintel and the original portal hinges behind it (Fig. 43) also survives. The jamb on the opposite side was apparently cut away when the portal was widened to fit Buontalenti's façade in the new axis of the present church. Also in place (Fig. 42) are the pointed windows in the aisles and the oculus. On the basis of the fixed relationships of the old portal, the aisle windows and the aisle roof line, it appears that the oculus in the fresco is identical *not* with the upper of the two to be

82. Paatz v, p. 343 n. 142a.

83. For a lengthy discussion of the problem "Nicola Pisano Architetto" cf. G. Nicco Fasola, *Nicola Pisano*, pp. 175f. See also Baldaccini 1951-1952, pp. 78f.; K. Frey, *Vasari-Vite*, 1911, pp. 802f., W. Krönig, "Nicola Pisano," 1953, *passim*.

84. K. Frey, *Vasari-Vite*, pp. 575, 824f.; so still Paatz v, p. 268. For Frey's earlier views, cf. the literature cited in note 67 supra.

85. Cf. Salmi, pls. 30, 123, 124, 140, 144, 151, 225, et al.

86. I would like to acknowledge my obligation to Dr. Eve Borsook for helpful comments concerning the state of the Sassetti Chapel frescoes. Cf. also E. Borsook, *The Mural Painters of Tuscany*, London, 1960, pp. 159-160.

87. The southern pilaster strip is still *in situ*, behind the Buontalenti façade, accessible from the space over the vaults under the roof of the southern side chapels. Its existence suggests that other fragments of the pre-1592 façade may also have survived behind the cover of the present façade.

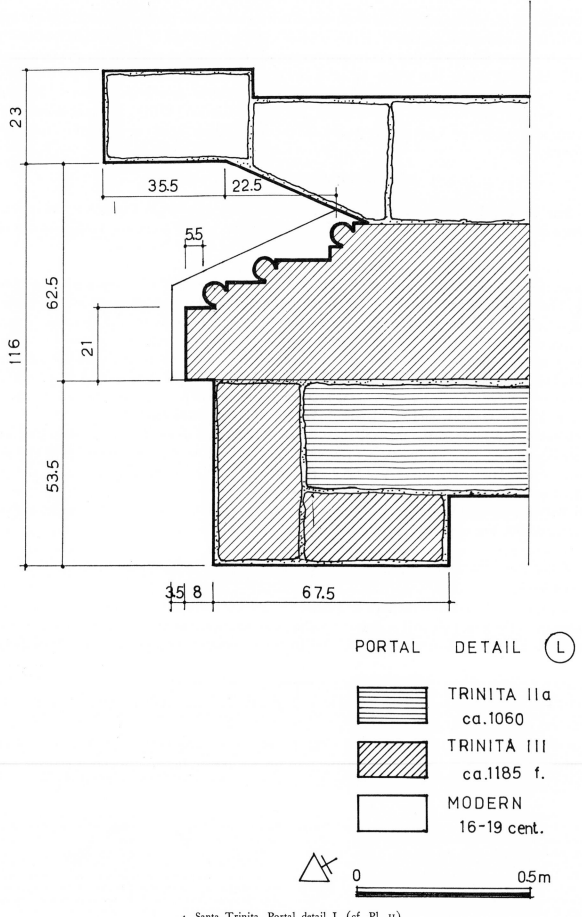

PORTAL   DETAIL   Ⓛ

TRINITA IIa
ca.1060

TRINITA III
ca.1185 f.

MODERN
16-19 cent.

0   0.5 m

4. Santa Trinita, Portal detail L (cf. Pl. II)

seen on the interior (which was inserted during the nineteenth century restorations[88]), but with the *lower one* in the axis of Trinita I-II.

An arcaded façade of this type is unique in Florence, but no rarity in Pisa, Lucca, Pistoia and Pescia after the first half of the twelfth century.[89] Nardini,[90] Supino,[91] Cocchi,[92] Salmi,[93] Botto,[94] and Paatz[95] agreed on an early to mid-thirteenth century date for the fresco façade. Only Paatz and Baldaccini have commented on the surviving fragment of the portal; both dated it in the early to mid-thirteenth century.[96]

Most recent observers have felt that the façade in the fresco is not of one piece.[97] The upper parts of the aisles, including the pointed windows and the pilaster strips flanking the aisles and the nave, extending on either side and above the oculus,[98] as well as the upper section over the oculus appear to be contemporary with the existing church as it was before the Buontalenti demolitions. The lower part, including the portals, arcades and the oculus, can probably not be dated later than the middle of the thirteenth nor much before the middle of the twelfth century. Three factors are decisive: 1) the ground level of the lower part is at the present level; and 2) the width of the lower part is equal to the width of the existing nave and aisles. Thus it cannot have been the façade of Trinita II, which was almost 4m narrower and 1.48m below the present level. 3) On the other hand, much lower in height and 25cm south of the axis of the Gothic church, the fresco façade was not an organic part of the present building either.

The elements façade (Fig. 9), visible on the interior since the restorations, also require renewed study. The exposed wall again appears to consist of *two distinct parts*. The lower central section extends four stone courses above the two small arched windows, while the upper part includes the lower oculus. Both parts center on the old (Trinita I-II) axis. The character of the masonry and the details confirm an eleventh century origin for the lower section. Originally extending down to the —1.48m level, it is evidently a large fragment, but not the whole, of the Trinita II façade.

There is a rough break on both sides of the center section, indicating the juncture of the arcade and, we may assume, the clerestory wall of Trinita II with the façade. The rough surface continues upward for about 30-40cm above the line of regular stone masonry marking the lower central part of the façade wall. The upper part of the façade wall is executed in smooth but irregular masonry of smaller and larger blocks. While it remains unclear what prompted the restorers to draw a gable line above the lower oculus, it may be supposed that this line was suggested by the apparent juncture with different masonry that marks the still further upward enlargement of the building. The notched indentations flanking the oculus suggest that the Trinita II clerestory wall was raised to the new roof line and loosely bound into the façade extension (Figs. 9, 10).

The heights of the side aisles of these two successive phases can be partially reconstructed from the wall fragment just to the south of the northern arcade line of Trinita II (Fig. 9). The side aisle and nave masonry matches and binds as far as a level a little less than halfway up the decorative blind niches in the central section. At this level a junction with irregular, non-binding masonry identical with that of the nave extension indicates the upward extension of the side aisle as well. Traces of small round windows are partially visible under modern plaster to the left and

88. Cf. note 25 supra.

89. Salmi, *passim*.

90. A. Nardini Despotti Mospignotti, *Il Duomo di San Giovanni*, p. 139 n. 2.

91. I. B. Supino, *Gli albori del arte fiorentina*, p. 132.

92. Cocchi, *Chiese*, pp. 167f.

93. Salmi, p. 39 n. 25.

94. Botto, 1938, p. 4 n. 1.

95. Paatz v, p. 268.

96. Paatz's discussion is unclear on this point. He appears to consider the central portal in the fresco as part of the

Romanesque church (Paatz v, pp. 267-268), but then he describes the jamb fragment as an addition of the 1251f. period (*ibid.*, p. 269).

97. So, e.g., K. Frey, *Vasari-Vite*, p. 825; A. Nardini, *op.cit.*, p. 139 n. 2; I. B. Supino, *op.cit.*, 1906, p. 132; Baldaccini, 1950; Paatz v, pp. 267-269.

98. Concerning the 19th century insertion of the present upper oculus visible on the interior, cf. note 25 supra. Our reconstruction of the Trinita III façade in text figs. 5 and 6 is based on the assumption that the Trinita III clerestory was also flanked by pilaster strips.

right of the Gothic pilasters abutting the façade. (Fig. 42) They are above the level of regular, binding masonry and are evidently also part of the upward extension of the Trinita II façade.[99]

The massive buttress-like jambs of the center portal comprise the final element in the masonry mélange of the interior façade. Since this portal was cut into the Trinita II façade when the new level was created and, presumably, the upper extension was made, it is not surprising that the jambs do not bind with the older masonry.[100]

The evidence of the interior and exterior façade elevations suggests that these alterations to the Trinita II façade postdate the eleventh century and predate the fourteenth century. This third phase may be considered as Trinita III, while the fourteenth century building now becomes Trinita IV.

Trinita II was much lower than has been believed (cf. text fig. 5); it was similar to its nearby contemporary, Santi Apostoli. Its gable rose from a level corresponding to the indicated line above the arched windows. Masonry identical with the lower part must have originally filled the gable triangle and may even have contained an upper window. This gable was leveled to the indicated line when the Trinita III façade was built. This façade extended at least to the height of the wall now exposed on the interior and contained a new (the lower) oculus shown in the fresco façade and still *in situ*. When the new level was created and the church made higher, it was also widened to an extent corresponding to the present nave and side aisles. This is apparent from the relationship of the arcades in the fresco façade to the nave and aisles of Trinita IV. The last arcade on either side does not appear to be a "later addition" as has been suggested.[101] The traces of an upward extension of the Trinita II clerestory walls in the succeeding period suggest that the nave diameter of Trinita III remained identical with Trinita II although the side aisles were widened.

When the Trinita III façade was absorbed into Trinita IV and extended yet further upward to cover the new higher elevation of the vaulted fourteenth century building, the pilaster strips flanking the side aisles and the clerestory visible in the fresco (Fig. 4) were added.[102] The pilaster strips flanking the upper part of the nave of the fresco façade closed the gap between the Trinita III arcaded façade and the clerestory walls of the wider nave of Trinita IV (text fig. 5). The slight (25cm) shift in axis is of minor importance and could have been overcome by making the northern flanking pilaster strips of aisle and clerestory slightly wider than their southern counterparts. The four unhomogeneous chapels flanking the southern aisle of Trinita IV were built against Trinita III at various times before 1362 and absorbed into the present building together with the older façade.

The evidence of changing levels, width and height implied by the façade walls may be interpreted in terms of a church behind that façade. What was the occasion for this enlargement? If our surmise about the *casa solariata* wall is well founded, then Trinita II was still in existence in 1124.[103] By 1178, however, the situation of the monastery, formerly outside the walls, had changed entirely. In that year the church received the *jus parrocchiale*, a few years after it was enclosed in the expanded city wall. Between 1188 and 1198 the parish was further enlarged.[104] Under these circumstances a larger church building, at the level of the newly created street and piazza in front of it, would appear to have been desirable.

EXCAVATIONS 1957-1958

What physical evidence remains to corroborate the existence of our postulated Trinita III behind

99. I am indebted to Dr. Friedrich Oswald for advice in the analysis of the interior façade masonry. In particular, Dr. Oswald pointed out the significance of the notched indentations to either side of the lower oculus and convinced me that the Trinita III nave had the same width as Trinita II.

100. Cf. also Paatz v, pp. 267, 340 n. 127.

101. Baldaccini, 1951-1952, p. 59 n. 6. Similarly Paatz v, p. 269: "Vergrösserung der zu übernehmenden romanischen Fassade."

102. Cf. note 98.

103. Cf. p. 18 supra.

104. Cf. note 15 supra.

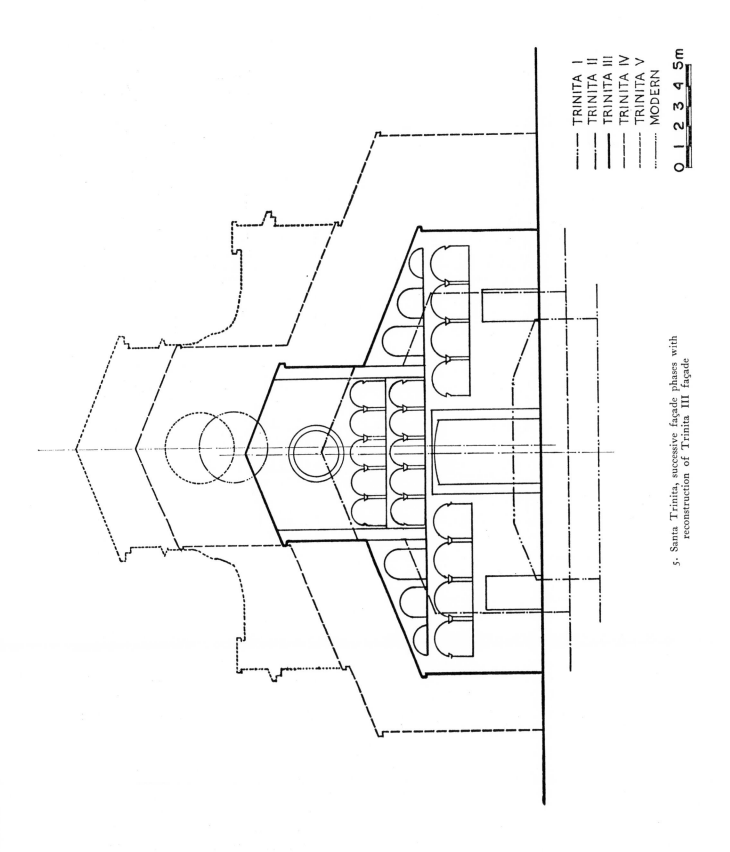

5. Santa Trinita, successive façade phases with reconstruction of Trinita III façade

TRINITA I
TRINITA II
TRINITA III
TRINITA IV
TRINITA V
MODERN

0 1 2 3 4 5m

6. Trinita III, reconstruction in present setting

the façade line? It was to shed light on this question as well as to clear up the problems surrounding the earlier buildings that the excavations of 1957 and 1958 were undertaken.

Our basic assumptions, namely that the overall width and level of Trinita III equaled Trinita IV (with a minimal difference of axes), combined with our contingent hypothesis that the first four southern chapels were added to the side-aisle walls of our postulated Trinita III, made it obvious just where test excavations were to be made: under and slightly in front of the steps leading to the chapels at a number of points on either side.

In October, 1957, a test trench was dug in front of the second left (southern) side chapel (Pl. II, A). This point was chosen because a foundation wall in front of this chapel would confirm both the existence of Trinita III and the postulation that the first four southern chapels (apparently built before the rest of Trinita IV) were not originally part of, but later additions to, Trinita III.

As elsewhere, the modern (1885f.) brick pavement, laid *a spina di pesce*, is supported to a depth of .45-.50m by a layer of river stones and dry earth contemporary with the pavement. The steps leading to the side chapels, also completely renewed in the late nineteenth century restorations, are laid on a 20cm high underpinning of bricks and cement. Below this level a layer of irregularly projecting stones appears to indicate a previous pavement level, 20cm under the present pavement, the existence of which Castellazzi reported in 1885 (Fig. 37).[105] Since he did not describe his findings in detail, it must remain uncertain whether more positive evidence of a pavement was then visible. For practical reasons both the modern steps and their immediate underpinnings were left in place.

At a depth of .50m, 40cm under the front line of the steps, a wall came to light (25-56cm equals the axis differential between Trinita I-III and Trinita IV). This wall was uncovered to a depth of about 1.20m and to a length of roughly 2.45m, i.e., up to a point under the center axis of the chapel (Pl. II, A; Figs. 37, 38). The masonry consists of fairly regular blocks, averaging 12-15cm in height and 25-30cm in length. The mortar joints average 3.5-4.5cm. The stones are cut roughly even, but not finished smooth. Occasional smooth-cut blocks may be spoils from another building (probably Trinita II). There are rare instances of thin, small brick (cf. also Appendix I).

The search for the Trinita III side wall on the northern flank was carried on during the campaign of February-March, 1958. It was discovered in excavation D extending from the fourth to the second right-hand chapels, 34cm in front of and extending partially under the chapel steps (Figs. 34-36, 39, 40, Pls. II, D; VI). The composition of its masonry—roughly hewn blocks of varying sizes with occasional smoothly hewn blocks as well as rare thin brick fragments and 2-3cm thick mortar joints—corresponds to the foundation found on the south side of the church. This wall extends nearly 5m up to a point 1.52m west of the pilaster between the second and third side chapels. Here it runs up against and, for about another 1.50m, over the earlier casa solariata wall (Pl. VI) (cf. p. 18 supra), which appears to have been partly re-utilized as a foundation for the Trinita III side wall. The incomplete nature of the investigation of the casa solariata wall prohibits final conclusions. The position of the northern foundation wall .34m in front of the chapel steps and that of the southern wall .40m under the steps, corresponds with the change of axis between Trinita III and IV.

With the side walls determined, it appears that the aisles of Trinita III were slightly wider than its nave, whose width was determined by that of Trinita II. This phenomenon is not unique in the Toscana in the twelfth and thirteenth centuries.[106]

In the light of these observations the irregular piece of wall continuing on the line of the Trinita II end wall (Pls. II, V, Fig. 29) (cf. p. 15 supra) gains in significance. It may be interpreted as the foundation of an extension of the Trinita II end wall to close the side aisle of Trinita III at the new (±0.00m) level. According to this hypothesis, it would follow that the trefoil enclosing walls of Trinita I remained as the choir of the new wider and higher Trinita III. Whether

105. G. Castellazzi, S. Trinita, pp. 23f. Paatz V, pp. 269-270. Like so many details, small and large, concerning the history of this church, the question of the pavements has led to confusion and misunderstandings. Castellazzi reported that both the pavement remains he found at the present level (i.e., 40cm under the then-existing level of 1820) and traces of yet another "third" pavement, found yet 20cm further down, were laid "a spina di pesce." Franceschini, in other respects a 100 per cent partisan of Castellazzi's restoration plans (cf. literature cited in note 24 supra) objected (Nuovo osservatore, 1885, p. 47 n. 1, p. 199 and S. Trinita, 1898) that the traces of the pavements found at the present level and 20cm below did not justify reconstruction of the new pavement at the present level a spina di pesce. Both the "second" and "third" pavements were "mattonato di foggia commune come quello che gli fu sopramesso." He complicated the discussion by writing (1885) of "due impiantiti sopra quel terzo che va ora a sparire," but the sense of the passage makes it clear that by quel terzo he meant the uppermost one of 1820 which

was about to be demolished. In the reprint of his 1885 article in his booklet of 1898, he corrected sopra to sotto without remarking on it. Paatz, perhaps confused by Franceschini's error or by Castellazzi's vague use of the terms secondo piano and terzo piano, referring variously to either the present level or the one 20cm below it (S. Trinita, 1887, pp. 23f.), finally took Franceschini's remarks to refer to the pavement of the 11th century basilica, 1.48m under the present level (Paatz V, p. 267). Actually, none of the various discussions about the pavements and levels ever mentioned the discovery of the 11th century pavement or its possible composition. Franceschini's objection to the spina di pesce pavement reconstruction should be given some credence. He himself reported in his article of 1885 that Castellazzi (probably anxious to enlist him on his side) had personally shown him around the church while the pavement excavations were going on, i.e., sometime before the "Sotto-Commissione di Vigilanza" went into action.

106. Cf. the Duomo in Carrara and the Pieve in Calci (Salmi, pls. LXIX and LXXI).

the crypt remained accessible or was filled in is, of course, a matter of pure speculation. It should be noted, however, that a crypt is never referred to in the various documents after 1200.

Work was continued in the complex of cellar rooms under the choir and side chapels (Pl. VII). This complex dates from about 1388f.[107] Various internal changes, including the thin, irregular partition walls, replastering and redecoration, were made in the eighteenth and nineteenth centuries. The level is about 2.50m under level ±0.00m of Trinita IV. Tests were made at the extreme eastern line of the cellar complex at a point under the altar platform at the top of the modern steps leading to the choir. On this line the complex is closed off by a straight wall parallel to the transept axis. The masonry of this wall (now covered with plaster) is smooth, consisting of large stone blocks mixed freely with large bricks. Comparison with the clerestory masonry around the transept (cf. pp. 35f.) as well as the documented date of the cellar complex, suggest that this wall was built in the later fourteenth century.

Fifteen to thirty-five centimeters under the irregular modern floor level of the underground rooms, this straight wall is founded on another which projects between 5-10cm (text fig. 7; Fig. 41). Its masonry corresponds exactly to the foundation walls we have connected with Trinita III, consisting of large (up to 10 x 65cm) ashlars with very rare brick fragments. This wall was excavated to about 2.50m under the cellar level. Like the wall in front of the Trecento chapels, this wall has been pierced at a number of points at which flat brick arches have been inserted. Skeletal remains were found at all levels in front of the wall and under the arches.

The foundation wall was followed south in a series of trenches to a point precisely in line with the southern side wall of Trinita III (Pl. II; text fig. 7). Here it breaks off while the fourteenth century wall over it continues onward about 3m further to close off the room under the second southern flanking transept chapel on its own foundations, which are of the same kind of masonry as the wall above and do not go down more than 1m under the cellar level (Fig. 41). A test of the width of the older wall at its end revealed a diameter of .74m, perhaps indicative of the width of the Trinita III side foundation which, being wholly or partially under the chapel steps, could not be satisfactorily measured. The character of the masonry of this wall, and the fact that its southern end corresponds precisely to the southern limit of Trinita III, suggest a relationship, though its purpose is obscure. It may be part of the monastery complex, supposed to have been to the west of the church.[108]

A report dated 1388 states: "Campanile vecchio della chiesa si disfa."[109] It does not specify just where the old tower was and, of course, it also leaves open the question of its date. A number of other documentary reports connected with the building of Trinita IV in the years around 1390, however, allow some speculation on these points. Thus, we know that the passageway leading from the northern transept wing to the Via del Parione was built in 1394[110] while the Ardinghelli Chapel in the northern corner between the transept and the nave (Fig. 7) was probably erected around 1393.[111] The long delay in the completion of this end of the transept until just after the documented demolition of the old bell tower, as well as irregularities in the plan at this point, suggest that the site of the old campanile was in the eastern corner of the transept wing, approximately on the site of the Ardinghelli Chapel near the northwestern corner of Trinita III.

TRINITA III: SUMMARY

The existence of Trinita III, its level and the position of its side and façade walls have been

107. Cf. Paatz V, pp. 285, 389 n. 387. These rooms were begun in 1388 apparently shortly after the old campanile was demolished.

108. Botto, 1938, p. 2.

109. Paatz V, p. 332 n. 57.

110. Paatz V, pp. 332 n. 60, 351 n. 190. The inner and outer portals of this *androne* and the flanking room behind the Ardinghelli Chapel (all marked with the Ardinghelli coat-of-arms) appear to be part of a later reworking, about 1420, probably by the Michelozzo shop (cf. H. Saalman, "Montepulciano," p. 45).

111. Paatz V, pp. 261, 332 n. 59.

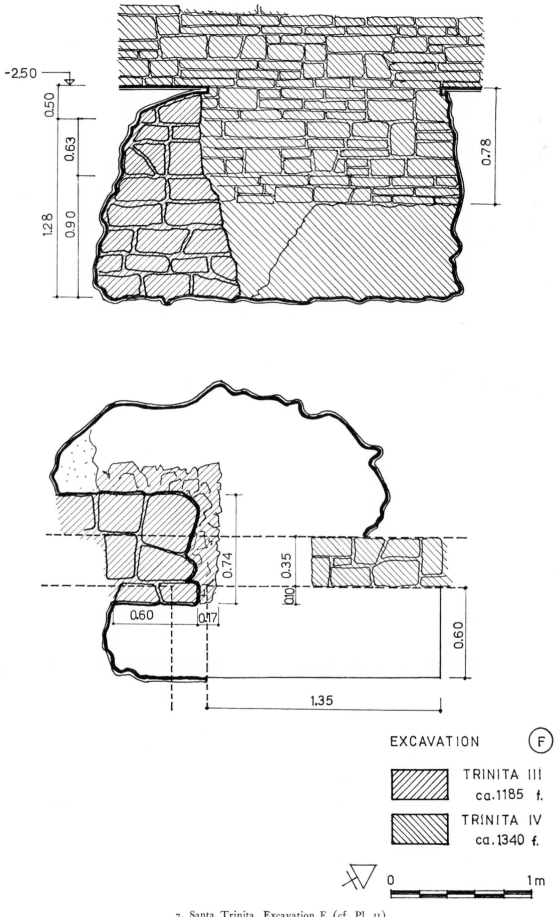

7. Santa Trinita, Excavation F (cf. Pl. II)

established. Traces on the façade interior suggest that the nave of Trinita III was no wider than that of Trinita II and that its aisles were slightly wider than the nave. The disposition of the western end remains somewhat uncertain, but its reconstruction as a wider and higher repetition of Trinita II at a new level, with the trefoil walls of Trinita I surviving as its choir, probably without crypt, may be proposed.

It was to this building that the four shallow southern chapels would appear to have been attached at various successive times. During the recent (1961-1962) restoration of the Salimbeni Chapel (fourth northern) a fragment of older masonry was uncovered in the northern (outer) wall of the chapel. It included a 2.15m high by .68m wide arched splay window, 14.5cm wide on the outside, with its axis .54m east of the present chapel axis (Pl. 11). If, as may be supposed, this window formed part of yet another chapel attached to Trinita III, the chapel, which may be one of those demolished during the course of the fourteenth century reconstruction,[112] was well within the extent of our proposed Trinita III.[113]

The disposition of the pre-Trinita IV chapels, finally, suggests (but by no means proves) that the intercolumniations of the Trinita III arcade equaled those of Trinita IV except for a shorter bay in front of the trefoil choir.[114]

112. Paatz V, pp. 259, 322 n. 20.

113. I am obligated to Dr. Hannelore Glasser for bringing this find to my attention and providing the measurements, assisted also by Dott. Berta Leggeri.

114. For our reconstruction of the Trinita II arcade cf. text figs. 2 and 3 and note 58 supra. The restrictions imposed on our investigations by the clergy prevented any excavation within the nave. It was impossible, therefore, to ascertain the precise location of either the Trinita II or Trinita III nave supports. While the Trinita II intercolumniations can be calculated by comparison with Santi Apostoli (cf. note 58), the dimensions of the Trinita III bays remain undetermined. With a Trinita III nave width apparently equal to that of Trinita II, the hypothetical final members of the Trinita III arcades, presumably abutting Trinita I at the ±0.00m level, would have been imposed directly on the truncated Trinita II trefoil piers in front of Trinita I.

CHAPTER III

THE CHURCH THAT NICOLA PISANO DID NOT BUILD: SANTA TRINITA IV

THE existence of Trinita III appears established; its date of origin, however, is less certain. As long as incontrovertible documentary evidence is lacking, a date for those parts of the present church not clearly documented must be supported by an analysis of the membering and the masonry.

TWO HEAD CONSOLES

A pair of consoles in the corners between the façade and the wall of the side chapel bearing the ribs of the side-aisle vaults (Fig. 42) has presented problems of dating and attribution related to the Nicola Pisano question. Neither head is of the highest quality, but they do bear a resemblance to products of the Pisano school. The round bulk of the bearded chin and cheek, the straight heavy nose, the high prominent cheek bones, the deep-set eyes and bulging eye balls of the northern head (Fig. 46) may in fact be compared to the head of the Archangel Michael on the Pisan baptistery pulpit of 1260 as Paatz has done.[115] The parted lips and the stylization of the beard and hair of the southern head (Fig. 45) resemble the *Crucified Christ* in the Siena Pulpit.[116] The agonized expression parallels those of the damned in the Siena *Last Judgment*.[117] The stylized forehead curls are rare in Nicola's work, but may be seen in the first kneeling king of the Pisa baptistery *Adoration of the Magi*.[118] The busts as such are comparable to those supporting the holy-water font in San Giovanni fuorcivitas in Pistoia.[119] Caryatid or head consoles in various forms occur in Pisa (baptistery, Camposanto)[120] and in Florence (Santa Maria Novella,[121] and the Badia[122]).

While the style of the consoles does not contradict a mid-thirteenth century origin, their connection with the vaulting system creates some problems. The block of which the southern bust is a part reaches up some 15cm over the crown of the head. The impost does not fit exactly over the block and is not of one piece with it (Figs. 42, 43). The form of the impost can be matched by others around the church, e.g., the imposts over the pilaster capitals flanking the Sassetti Chapel in the northern transept arm, which was not built before the last decade of the fourteenth century.[123]

The northern head does appear to be of one piece with the three-part impost over it (Fig. 46). But the impost, consisting of a fillet, a torus, and a chamfered cornice, all massively proportioned, has no parallel in the present church.

The two console busts are similar in kind, but apparently not a matched pair. It must be concluded that the date of the busts themselves is not indicative of the date when they were inserted in their present location, apparently when the fourteenth century vaults were built.[124] They have

115. Paatz V, pp. 280, 347 n. 173; *idem, Trecentoarchitektur*, p. 29 and figs. 42, 43; G. Nicco Fasola, "Induzioni su Nicola Pisano Architetto," p. 319, fig. 2.

116. E. Carli, *Nicola Pisano*, Milan-Florence, 1953, pl. 34.

117. *Ibid.*, pl. 37.

118. J. Pope-Hennessy, *Italian Gothic Sculpture*, New York, 1955, pl. 3.

119. A. Venturi, *Giovanni Pisano, Sein Leben und sein Werk*, Munich, 1927, pls. 10-12.

120. *Idem*, pl. 44 et al. W. Biehl, *Toskanische Plastik des frühen und hohen Mittelalters*, Leipzig, 1926, pl. 59.

121. W. Paatz, *Trecentoarchitektur*, figs. 8-9; E. Borsook, *The Mural Painters of Tuscany*, pl. 87.

122. U. Middeldorf and W. Paatz, "Die gotische Badia zu Florenz und ihr Erbauer Arnolfo di Cambio," *Mitt. Kunsthist. Inst. Florenz*, III, 1932, p. 500, fig. 6 (hereafter, Middeldorf and Paatz, "Badia"). The Florentine tradition of head consoles goes back to the Romanesque period, e.g., at San Jacopo oltr'Arno (W. Biehl, *op.cit.*, pls. 116-117); Pisa: Biehl, *op.cit.*, pl. 59.

123. Paatz V, pp. 332f. n. 60.

124. Cf. Paatz V, p. 348 n. 173. E. Marcucci, *Arte e Storia*, IV, 1885, p. 73, had already felt that even if the first three left-hand chapels were earlier, their vaults and those of the side aisles belong to the 14th century. K. Frey, in Thieme-Becker, II, p. 143, felt that the heads were reused pieces inserted when the vaults were built. Their rather battered and weathered condition suggests that these heads were previ-

two counterparts under the ribs of the vaults in the east and west corners of the southern transept wing. Neither of these can have been inserted before the last decade of the fourteenth century when the transept was completed. The one in the western corner (Fig. 56) resembles work recently attributed to Niccolo di Pietro Lamberti.[125]

CAPITAL STUDIES

A study of the capitals in late thirteenth-early fourteenth century Florentine architecture aiming at chronological definition faces considerable obstacles. The history of even the best-known buildings, e.g. the Palazzo del Podestà (Bargello), Santa Maria Novella, Santa Croce and Santa Maria del Fiore, is far from clarified. The columns and capitals of the upper loggia in the Bargello (Fig. 69), for example, are documented in 1320.[126] Those of the ground-floor arcade are similar while the outer masonry of ground floor, first floor *and* of the rear palace is so clearly of one piece (Fig. 70), that one wonders whether everything in back of the old 1254f. wing should not be considered as built in the documented period of 1296-1320 when greater sums than ever before were expended on the building.[127] The transept of Santa Maria Novella has been dated as early as 1246 while others feel that there is no reason to accept a date before 1279.[128] At Santa Croce the transept and some of its chapels appear to have been finished about 1310, but the nave represents a far from precisely dated repertory of capitals dating from the 1320's to the end of the fourteenth century.[129] The history of Santa Maria del Fiore has only recently been defined.[130] The piers and their capitals are well dated, all after 1357. The thirteenth and fourteenth century reconstructions of smaller buildings such as San Remigio,[131] Santa Maria Maggiore,[132] the Ognissanti,[133] and Santissima Annunziata[134] are poorly documented or wholly obscure. Some better defined complexes date after 1330. In others such as the 1254f. wing of the Bargello or the Badia (1284-1310),[135] there are no comparable capitals, or none remain. There is, in a word, little well-dated material with which the capitals of the present Santa Trinita may be compared. For the period before 1275, we must, in fact, look outside of Florence.

Of the pilaster capitals between the first four southern chapels, only one original fragment survives (on the pilaster between the third and fourth chapel; Fig. 47). The others are modern copies, evidently after the surviving fragment. Only one-half of the long side of the original capital remains. On the side toward the fourth chapel it is adjoined by a short fragment similar in type, but different in details. The part of the pilaster facing the interior of the fourth chapel is

ously used elsewhere, perhaps in similar fashion as the familiar heads on the corners of the "Scarsella" at San Giovanni (Salmi, p. 54; Paatz II, p. 185, p. 236 n. 82).

125. C. Seymour, "The Younger Masters of the First Campaign of the Porta della Mandorla, 1391-1397," ART BULLETIN, XLI, 1959, pp. 1f.; see also M. Wundram, "Niccolo di Pietro Lamberti und die Florentiner Plastik um 1400," *Jahrbuch der Berliner Museen*, IV, 1962, pp. 78ff.

126. W. Paatz, "Zur Baugeschichte des Palazzo del Podestà (Bargello) in Florenz," *Mitt. Kunsthist. Inst. Florenz*, III, 1932, pp. 318f., doc. 39 (hereafter, Paatz, "Bargello").

127. Paatz has suggested that the ground-floor loggia, its columns and its surrounding walls were built about 1280-1285 ("Bargello," pp. 302f.). This view may be the result of a misinterpretation of his docs. 10 and 16 (p. 316). The "logia" and "portici" referred to in 1286 and 1292 (in the latter year as "noviter facti" are modified both times by the words "seu verone." But a *verone* is not necessarily a loggia or a portico in the more usual sense. It may be an exterior platform on arcades, sometimes covered, at the top of a flight of steps in front of an upper entrance. Examples are numerous in surviving Romanesque town halls, e.g., in Umbria at Todi and Perugia; in Toscana: Massa Marittima (Pal. Pretorio, ca. 1230); San Gimigniano (Pal. nuovo del Podestà); Prato (Pal. Pretorio). Cf. also Michelangelo's Pal. Senatorio proj-

ect for the Capitoline Hill (J. Ackerman, *The Architecture of Michelangelo*, New York, 1961, p. 58, fig. 8). The front palace is referred to in 1320 as the "old palace" while the rear house is the "new palace" (Paatz, "Bargello," p. 319). Such terms may be ambiguous, but there is no firm indication that the rear house or the courtyard with its porticoes existed before the early 14th century. So already Limburger, *Gebäude von Florenz*, pp. 16-17; cf. also Saalman, "Montepulciano," p. 34 n. 31. Dr. Jürgen Paul in a recent Freiburg dissertation (*Die mittelalterlichen Kommunalpaläste in Italien*, Freiburg, 1963, pp. 210-216) suggests a sequence of events nearly identical with that indicated here.

128. Cf., e.g., R. Davidsohn, *Forschungen zur Geschichte von Florenz*, IV, Berlin, 1896-1908, pp. 466f. and note 179 below.

129. Paatz I, pp. 502-503.

130. Cf. H. Saalman, "Santa Maria del Fiore: 1294 to 1418," ART BULLETIN, XLVI, 1964, pp. 471ff.

131. Paatz V, pp. 5f.

132. Paatz III, pp. 615f.

133. Paatz IV, pp. 406f.

134. Paatz I, pp. 62f.

135. U. Middeldorf and W. Paatz, "Badia," pp. 422f.; Paatz I, pp. 264f.

modern. It is to be suspected that the smaller fragment is the only surviving part of one of the original capitals of the first three pilasters and that it was placed here during the nineteenth century restorations. Castellazzi[136] reported that these capitals were badly worn when he began his restorations.

Two and one-half leaf units cover the lower part of the remaining half of the long side of the surviving capital. Each unit consists of two thick, flat, deeply ribbed and pointed acanthus leaf halves which curve up and flare outward. The units are joined by little leaf tongues. An upper row of flat leaves, articulated by a single raised vertical rib, rises behind the lower leaf row and falls over in a short, ribbed, three-part leaf crest. Each upper leaf carries a dentil on which, in turn, the impost rests.

A comparison with the lush, voluminous, finely ribbed and pointed foliage of the column capitals bearing Nicola's pulpit in the Pisan baptistery[137] shows no apparent relationship whatever. The leaves of various capitals around the transept of Santa Maria Novella[138] are divided into finely articulated units. A short leaf finger often folds over at the bottom of a leaf into a "leaf eye." The leaves spring up straight, then fold forward and then curve upward again. In other examples in the choir chapels of Santa Maria Novella,[139] deeply ribbed acanthus leaves are sometimes topped by noodle-like volute spirals. Whether 1246 or 1279, these capitals bear no resemblance in type or form to the Trinita capital. The leaves of three figured capitals in the Museo Nazionale in Florence, believed to have come from the Badia (1284f.) are too poorly preserved to serve as an adequate comparison,[140] but the leaf type has no visible relationship to the Trinita capital. Turning to capitals of the ground-floor arcade in the Bargello *cortile* (Fig. 69), which I am inclined to date between 1316 and 1320[141] (i.e., contemporary with the capitals of the documented upper loggia arcade), brings us closer to a solution. The lower leaf row of the southeastern corner pier capital is composed of flat, ribbed units that flare outward while the upper row consists of flat leaves, with a single raised center rib and crests that closely resemble the Trinita capital. But the lower leaf row is flatter, less deeply incised and undercut than in our capital. A console capital in the southern upper loggia, inserted into the wall of the old mid-thirteenth century Bargello wing, is part of the vaulting system that was added to this loggia between 1332 and 1346 (Fig. 48).[142] It seems most nearly identical with our capital. Fleshy, deeply ribbed lower leaf units flare up and out around the three sides of the polygonal capital. The units are joined by short leaf tongues. The upper flat leaves, each with a single raised vertical rib, curl over into ribbed three-part leaf crests. As with the Trinita capital, the outer sections of the leaf crests spiral inward while the central part points downward. A pilaster capital between the Bardi and Peruzzi Chapels in the transept of Santa Croce (about 1310)[143] and the third northern nave pier capital from the transept have an upper leaf row with the same characteristics. The pier capital is datable between about 1330 and 1341.[144] The crests of the Bargello capital carry no dentils and the abacus is not chamfered as at Santa Trinita, consisting of a cyma and a fillet; but this does not materially alter the close relationship in form and style between the two capitals. It seems, then, that a date between about 1330 and 1350 is considerably closer to the mark than one in mid-thirteenth century.

Paatz counted the capitals of the first three southern nave piers (Fig. 49) as part of a first (1250-1327) building period and coupled them with the console capitals over the first three southern and northern side chapels (Figs. 51, 53). Botto dated the first three southern pier capitals *only* ca. 1280, i.e., later than the "early" capitals, but before the 1362f. period. Paatz

136. G. Castellazzi, *S. Trinita*, p. 33. Cf. Paatz v, p. 347 n. 172.

137. A. Venturi, *Giovanni Pisano*, pl. 5; J. Pope-Hennessy, *Italian Gothic Sculpture*, pl. 1.

138. Paatz, *Trecentoarchitektur*, figs. 17-21.

139. *Ibid.*, fig. 10; E. Borsook, *The Mural Painters of Tuscany*, pl. 87.

140. U. Middeldorf and W. Paatz, "Badia," figs. 13, 14, 16.

141. W. Paatz, "Bargello," p. 307, fig. 13.

142. *Ibid.*, p. 311, fig. 16.

143. Paatz, *Trecentoarchitektur*, fig. 81.

144. *Ibid.*, fig. 77; cf. also Paatz I, p. 500.

is perfectly right in seeing both the pier and console capitals in question as a group.[145] But can they be dated 1280f.? The northern chapels, over which some of the console capitals in this group are found, were not built before 1362f.[146] All of the capitals in this group are of the same type, consisting of a lower row of flat, irregularly pointed leaves furrowed by deep, freely curving rib incisions. Elongated leaves of similar character grow up behind the first row. The central leaf is fairly straight, but the other leaves swing freely in elegant S-curves. The *calathos* core is visible, the leaves appear only loosely attached to the core and are deeply undercut (Figs. 49, 51, 53). The three pilaster capitals between the first four northern chapels (Fig. 52) and the façade pilaster and the third and fourth pier capitals of the northern nave arcade (Figs. 5, 8, 9) form a closely related group whose leaves are less deeply undercut and flatter. The capitals between the northern chapels have only a single leaf row. Leafy volutes grow out behind the lower leaves, turned toward each other at a sharp angle. They have parallels in the capitals of the Loggia del Bigallo, built in the years 1352-1361.[147] Capitals with loosely applied, freely curving leaves, complete with dentils under the imposts and base profiles resembling those of Santa Trinita may be found in the Chiostro Verde of Santa Maria Novella, dated ca. 1344-1360 and Or San Michele (ca. 1350-1357).[148]

The capitals of the last two piers on either side of the nave (Figs. 5, 6, 54) form a group characterized by a double row of lush, agitated foliage. The tips are massive and rounded and curl outward into clumps. Similar capitals and similar base profiles characterize the nave piers of Santa Maria del Fiore, designed by Francesco Talenti in 1357, executed in the fifteen years thereafter and of influence on the style of Francesco's son, Simone Talenti, in the 1370's.[149]

The capitals of the clerestory, some with unribbed leaves (*foglie d'acqua*) (Fig. 55), are of similar kind while the capitals around the transept are very varied. Some continue the forms of the earlier nave capitals (e.g. Fig. 7), some are of yet other types. The lower and upper capitals flanking the choir chapel (Fig. 5) are characteristic of this group. They are paralleled by capitals in the Castellani Chapel in Santa Croce (after 1383),[150] in Santissima Annunziata,[151] on the portal of San Carlo Borromeo (formerly San Michele)[152] and the Porta dei Canonici at Santa Maria del Fiore (last quarter of the fourteenth century).[153]

The first three southern pier capitals are rectangular (roughly 2:1). All the other nave pier capitals are higher, approaching a square shape. A change in plan evidently took place and a similar break occurs in the clerestory masonry above.[154]

We have, then, three major groups of capitals. They indicate three building phases, all in the fourteenth century: (1) 1330-1350: first four southern chapels; (2) 1350-1370: nave piers of first three bays on either side and first four northern chapels; (3) last quarter of the fourteenth century: clerestory and transept with chapels, last nave bay and last side-aisle chapels on either side.

With this analysis in mind, we may be able to arrive at a new chronology for Trinita IV. The only surviving pilaster capital of the first four southern chapels is different and apparently earlier than all other existing capitals. This fact may indicate that these chapels, which were in existence when the new project was begun,[155] were the first to be provided with pilasters and capitals in the process of adapting them to the system of a planned new church.

The date when this project was conceived is not documented. Beginning in the early 1360's,

145. Paatz V, p. 349 n. 175.

146. Cf. Paatz V, p. 349 n. 176.

147. Paatz I, pp. 371f. Cf. H. Saalman, "The Bigallo: The Oratory and Residence of the Compagnia del Bigallo e della Misericordia in Florence" (in preparation).

148. Paatz III, pp. 670f.; IV, p. 483; E. Borsook, *op.cit.*, pls. 39, 54.

149. Paatz III, p. 445 n. 66. Saalman, "Santa Maria del Fiore, pp. 480ff., fig. 9.

150. Paatz I, p. 644 n. 267.

151. W. Lotz, "Michelozzo's Umbau der SS. Annunziata in Florenz," *Mitt. Kunsthist. Inst. Florenz*, V, 1940, p. 411.

152. Paatz I, pp. 411f.

153. Paatz III, p. 351.

154. Another indication of change in process of building: higher springing points of the nave vaults and correspondingly longer pilasters in the last nave bay (Pl. III).

155. Cf. note 77 supra.

a series of testaments of wealthy parishioners provide funds for new chapels to be built along the northern aisle. The transept and its chapels are not documented until later.

Two elements alone may give an indication of the date when the new church was begun. One is the date 1327 reported by Niccolini[156] when Pope John XXII is supposed to have made a consecration at the church. Another is a seventeenth century inscription in the first southern chapel (Strozzi), claiming that the chapel was *extructum* in 1340.[157] While Paatz[158] attached no significance to either of these dates, particularly the inscription, perhaps based on family records, it might be suggested, if only tentatively, that the reconstruction of the church was inaugurated in the late 1320's and that active work in the already existing chapels on the southern side was begun some ten years later.

The capitals of the first three southern nave piers and the southern façade pilaster (Figs. 8, 42) form a second group. These capitals appear to be contemporary with the console capitals above the first four chapels on *either* side (Figs. 51, 53).[159] The pilaster capitals of the first four northern chapels and of the third and fourth northern piers form another category within the second group, somewhat different in type, but of similar vintage. Because of the change from rectangular to roughly square capitals in the nave, it would seem that the first three southern piers and the other capitals in their group represent a somewhat earlier building phase. Stylistically they all fall into the years 1350-1370, but since the pilaster capitals between the right-hand chapels are probably not earlier than the chapels themselves, i.e., not before 1362f., a second building period may be postulated between about 1362 and 1370.[160]

At this point an extended interruption seems to have taken place, because the style of the pier capitals in the last two nave bays (Fig. 54) (derived from Santa Maria del Fiore), of the transept capitals (Fig. 7), and those of the last chapels on either side (none of the latter capitals are originals) is clearly that of the years after 1375. These capitals mark the final building phase, which extends into the early fifteenth century, a period also amply documented by written records.[161]

MASONRY STUDIES

A similar sequence of events can be deduced from an examination of the Trinita IV masonry visible at the clerestory level. The difficulties confronting capital studies in this period are also faced in masonry studies. A comparative study of thirteenth and fourteenth century masonry in various Florentine buildings suggests, however, that none of the masonry in the clerestory walls need necessarily be before the second quarter of the fourteenth century.[162]

In evidence we submit detail photographs of masonry from the Badia of Florence (1284f.),[163] Santa Maria Novella (1379f.?), the Palazzo del Podestà (Bargello, 1296-1320?) and parts of the third circle city wall on the southern side of the Arno, which was begun in 1324 (Figs. 65-68, 70).[164] It cannot be said that such comparisons lead to a definitive chronology of Florentine masonry technique in this period. If anything, the results (1324f. city wall) favor a fourteenth century date for the apparently "early" masonry fragment over the second and third southern nave arcade.

Nineteenth century reports commenting on the restorations stated that in the 1880's there were

156. Cf. p. 4 supra.
157. A. Cocchi, *Chiese*, p. 188.
158. Paatz V, p. 377 n. 309.
159. But cf. Paatz V, pp. 280-281.
160. Documents concerning the chapels: Paatz V, p. 260 and notes.
161. Cf. Paatz V, pp. 280-281, 350 n. 18.
162. Paatz's observations (V, pp. 273-275, 343-344 nn. 146-153) and conclusions concerning the clerestory masonry are briefly the following: *Southern clerestory*: first bay: not sure,

but probably originally 13th century, reworked in the 14th century; second and third bay: mid-13th century to about 1300; narrow upper strip under the roof line: probably a late 14th century addition. *All other clerestory masonry and choir chapel wall*: later 14th-15th century.
163. U. Middeldorf and W. Paatz, "Badia," pp. 422f.; Paatz I, pp. 264f.
164. G. Villani, *Cronica*, IX, 257. R. Davidsohn, *Forschungen*, IV, pp. 450f.

round windows in the bays over the first southern and first and second northern side chapels.[165] It is thus beyond question and obvious from their appearance (Fig. 58) that these parts are restorations of the late nineteenth century.[166] The narrow strip under the roof line (Figs. 59, 60) matches and binds with the late nineteenth century masonry of the first southern bay and must be connected with repairs to vaults and roofs suggested by the commission in 1885-1886.[167] The masonry of the second and third southern clerestory bay is, surely, the oldest visible (Fig. 59). However, there is no reason to date it much before the middle of the fourteenth century (cf. Figs. 65, 66). It may be noted that this piece of wall lies over the first three southern piers, which seem to belong to the early phase of the 1350-1370 building period. It was probably feasible to build the clerestory wall over these piers and to vault the first three side-aisle bays well in advance of other parts of the new church. The clearly marked building line between the third and fourth clerestory bays (Fig. 60) and the evidence of the documents indicates that the western part of the southern clerestory wall, the northern clerestory and the transept are more or less uniformly products of the late fourteenth century (Figs. 61, 62). It is possible, however, that the foundations of the transept and its chapels were laid around the western end of Trinita III somewhat earlier than the less than definite documents of the 1380's[168] indicate.

Nave widening: A survey of the church reveals that the nave widens progressively from east to west (Pl. 1). This widening is due to a progressive northward shift of the successive northern nave piers. The southern piers diverge only very slightly southward. The apparent reason for this shift seems to be the advantage of re-using the Trinita I wall as part of the pier foundation (Pl. 11). The foundation of the fourth northern nave pier does not penetrate, but is built against and over the Trinita I wall, as an examination of the corner next to the northern Trinita I window reveals (Fig. 20).

The present bell tower: The existing bell tower[169] as executed (Fig. 64) seems to be a curious mixture of afterthought and improvisation. Balanced rather audaciously over the northwestern corner of the choir chapel, it is actually founded on and built around the corner buttress of the choir chapel, which has been extended upward over the roof line. From here it rises up without particular distinction of form, crudely supported by two improvised arched buttresses and the straight upward extension of the gable of the choir chapel. About 6m above the roof of the adjoining transept chapel on the northern face of the campanile, a Donatellesque Madonna and Child relief of better than average quality,[170] now quite weathered, is inserted. The opening on the southern side was bricked up at a later period and various changes have been made in the upper parts of the tower. While the tower offers a poor comparison with the fine campaniles of the Ognissanti and Santa Maria Novella, the builders were clearly aware that it would be all but invisible from below. In the final building phase, all efforts seem to have been turned to finishing the church as quickly and cheaply as possible (cf. also Appendix I). The tower probably received its precarious perch on the church roof after it was decided not to demolish any further existing monastery buildings behind the church to make room for a free-standing campanile. It appears that the enlargement of the church had already encroached on the monastic quarters. This cramped situation was not improved until the revival of the Vallombrosians' fortunes during the sixteenth century and the building of the magnificent Buontalenti cloister (secularized during the Napoleonic period and now part of the University of Florence).

---

165. Castellazzi (*S. Trinita*, p. 74) curiously assumed that the circular windows were the original ones (following Santa Maria Novella?) while the pointed one was due to a later modification. His "reconstruction" of the façade and church prior to Buontalenti (*op.cit.*, plate facing p. 33) shows three(!) oculi followed by a pointed window in the northern clerestory. Cf. also Paatz v, p. 263.

166. Cf. also G. Carocci, *Arte e Storia*, v, 1886, p. 21,

and VIII, 1889, p. 119.

167. G. Carocci, *op.cit.*, 1886, p. 20. An examination of the interiors under the roof revealed that the roof line of nave, side aisles, and side chapels was raised about .90m during the restorations.

168. Paatz v, pp. 260, 328f. nn. 44-50.

169. Paatz v, p. 333 n. 62.

170. Paatz v, p. 275.

TENTATIVE CHRONOLOGY

To summarize briefly, we have roughly three fourteenth century phases: (1) a limited early one, possibly beginning *before* the middle of the century, during which the already existing side chapels were adapted for absorption into the new project;[171] (2) a second more extensive building period from about 1360 to 1370 during which the right-hand chapels and, probably, the first three nave bays were erected. Part of the clerestory and the vaulting of the first side-aisle bays may also have been finished in this early phase. This period ended in a long pause, beginning around 1370 and lasting until the middle 1370's or, perhaps, as late as the early 1380's, while the monks sought more money to finish the work; (3) from 1383 on, building continued without further interruptions until around 1405, when most of the church was finished. Completion of details followed.

A document of 1383 states that *ipsa ecclesia que erat verisimiliter dirutura magnam minabitur ruinam, fuit et est detecta et nisi per vestram providentiam faciendo provvisionem . . . ipsa ecclesia que tam est venerabilis et devota eius ruina sequetur.*[172] Botto used this text as an explanation for the demolition of his 1250-1327 church.[173] Paatz did not accept a "finished church," but connected the text to his 1258f. "fragment."[174] There is no difficulty whatever in relating the 1383 document to a church reconstruction begun twenty and more years before and left unfinished because of lack of funds some ten years earlier. Nothing is more likely than that parts already built were, in fact, *detecta*. Similar cries of woe and ruin are, furthermore, the rule in pleas of this kind, particularly when a lengthy interruption in building—and eight to thirteen years *is* a long time!—has gone before.[175]

TRINITA IV: A RE-EVALUATION

While a proper evaluation of Trinita IV depends on a prior consideration of predetermined elements, the *new* elements in plan, elevation, articulation and decoration absorb our interest in a final characterization. The plan and elevation, reflecting Santa Croce and the vaulted Santa Maria Novella, are fairly traditional in Trecento Florence. The addition of organically integrated side chapels on the flanks of the church represents a distinct innovation however. Yet these chapels are no architectural whim. They correspond to a pattern which became widespread all over Europe from about the middle of the thirteenth century. The chapels built between the buttresses of Notre-Dame of Paris after about 1235 are an early example of this phenomenon.[176] As we have seen, the first three chapels at the left of Trinita IV and some others whose exact location cannot now be established,[177] were later thirteenth to early fourteenth century additions to Trinita III. A number of wealthy families in the parish of Santa Trinita, the Spini, the Gianfigliazzi, the Strozzi, Davanzati, Scali, Compagni, Bartolini, Ardinghelli and Sercialli were in rapid ascendancy at the beginning of the fourteenth century. The demand for private chapels must have been pressing by the 1320's.

While the possibilities for creative imagination and "architectural expression" were obviously limited in Trecento practice, the design and execution of building details provided an outlet for artistic creativity. That the question of such details was not an unimportant matter at this time is best

---

171. Prof. Wolfgang Lotz observed a similar reconstruction of an earlier (in this case 13th century) church *without* side chapels in the third quarter of the 14th century at Santissima Annunziata (*Mitt. Kunsthist. Inst. Florenz*, V, 1940, p. 412). But see also A. Sabatini, "La Chiesa della SS. Annunziata di Firenze prima della ricostruzione Michelozziana," *Rivista d'Arte*, XII, 1940, pp. 229f. Some of the problems raised by these two articles still remain unresolved.

172. Paatz V, p. 330 n. 52 has *defecta*; but cf. Paatz V, p. 326 n. 35: ". . . ohne Dach." Arch. di St., Firenze, *Provvisioni*, 72, c. 72ᵛ: *detecta*.

173. Botto, 1938, pp. 10-12.

174. Paatz V, pp. 326 n. 35 and 330-331 n. 52.

175. An almost identically worded appeal to the Signoria concerning Or San Michele was made in 1350: *nisi subbito provideatur et compleantur uolte et copriatur, est periculum maximum ne armadurae propterea factae devastentur etc.* . . . (G. Gaye, *Carteggio inedito d'artisti dei secoli 14. 15. 16.*, Florence, 1839-1840, I, pp. 50-51). See also the speech of Prior Schiattesi of San Lorenzo in similar circumstances in 1440 (D. Moreni, *Continuazione delle memorie istoriche dell' Ambrosiana imperiale Basilica di S. Lorenzo in Firenze*, Florence, 1816, I, pp. 4f.).

176. M. Aubert, *Notre Dame de Paris*, Paris, 1920, pp. 37f. Cf. also the author's *Medieval Architecture*, p. 40.

177. Cf. pp. 4, 30 and notes 77, 112 supra.

illustrated by the well-known design competition for the nave piers of Santa Maria del Fiore in 1357.[178] The master or masters of Trinita IV found a solution for their nave piers which is an interesting combination of the various possibilities which had been developed in Florence up to the middle of the fourteenth century.

The closest relationship is to the system of Santa Maria Novella (1279f.), which is most similar in plan. Instead of quatrefoil piers, however, the Trinita pier is a combination of the square pier of Santa Maria Maggiore (mid-fourteenth century) with the through-running nave vault support of Santa Maria Novella and the Santa Croce pilaster.

The system of the western crossing pier pilasters flanking the main chapels is precisely that of Santa Croce (Fig. 5). The two eastern crossing piers are a curious combination (Fig. 7): toward the nave arcade and the side aisles they continue the square pier system of the nave; toward the crossing they run up to the springing point of the crossing arches in the form of half-cruciform piers resembling the piers of Santa Maria del Fiore. The quarter members in the angles carry the diagonal ribs while on the choir side the ribs rest directly on the corner of the crossing arch pilaster capital. The diagonal ribs of the first nave bay east of the crossing also spring from a corner of the north-south crossing arch pilaster capitals.

A certain lack of homogeneity is also evident in the side-aisle vaulting system (Figs. 5, 6). Square piers are set in front of the dividing walls between the side chapels; they are topped on the exposed sides by narrow rectangular leaf capitals of the type we have observed in the first three southern nave piers. While the east-west capitals may be said to carry the archivolts of the arches leading into the chapels, the capitals toward the aisles are quite non-functional.[179] The aisle vaults rest on rectangular leaf consoles set higher up at the level of the nave arcade capital.[180] The vault supports in the corner between the aisles and the façade are the two head consoles discussed above (pp. 31f.). A repetition of the through-running pilaster motif of the nave would surely have been an effective device, both logical and feasible. But an attempt to explain the side-aisle system as executed in terms of undocumented program changes, e.g., a suggestion that the vaulting system had not yet been planned when the piers and pilasters between the first three southern side chapels were inserted, would probably prove both unfounded and inadequate if the facts could be ascertained.

In the later building phase after about 1375, during which most of the nave piers and the transept appear to have been built, a wider capital with leaf and flower work characteristic of the last three decades of the century (e.g., at Or San Michele, San Michele Vecchio and the Loggia dei Signori) was adopted (Fig. 52).

The effect of the nave (Figs. 5, 9) with its square piers, its narrow intercolumniations, probably determined by the previous church, and its rather small nave windows high up under the vaults in the shallow clerestory, is one of static, enclosed space, articulated by massive, closely spaced solids. The whole is lightened by the slim ascending lines of the pilasters, carrying the nave vaults with their sleek polygonal ribs, and sweetened by the delicate lyricism of the late fourteenth century leaf-flower capitals and (originally) by the colors of the fresco decoration, of which only scattered fragments remain today.[181] There is little here which resembles the airy hall-like atmosphere of Santa Maria Novella and less that of Santa Croce.

178. Saalman, "Santa Maria del Fiore," p. 480.

179. Similar "non-functional" pilasters between the chapels flanking the main choir chapel of Santa Maria Novella (Paatz, *Trecentoarchitektur*, pl. 1). These have been interpreted as evidence of a "pre-1279" plan to vault the transept wings with adjoining rectangular bays (M. Wackernagel, *Mitt. Kunsthist. Inst. Florenz*, III, 1931, p. 351; Paatz III, pp. 684-685).

180. Paatz V, p. 346 n. 163.

181. The horizontal "strips" on the piers are almost certainly a figment of Comm. Castellazzi's imagination. The evidence for them, according to that cool-headed observer, E. Marcucci ("Restauri a Santa Trinita," *Arte e Storia*, IV, 1885, pp. 74f.) consisted in "Non . . . altra traccia nei pietrami delle colonne che una piccola zona diversamente scalpellata"—and that only on scattered piers. It should be remembered in this connection that the "roughing" of parts of the pilasters was for the purpose of preparing the stone for fresco painting. The frescoes, however, were not painted simultaneously and the preparation of two adjoining parts of

The transept presents a contrast (Fig. 7). With the rectangular arms to either side of the crossing and the large, originally all-open windows in the clerestory, with the high flanking chapels and the large main chapel, the transept is all wide, expansive vaulted space, similar to its prototype, the transept of Santa Maria Novella. Proportionally wider, though actually smaller, it is perhaps even more strongly reminiscent of the great hall of the Bargello (Fig. 71), vaulted in 1340-1345, just about the time when the reconstruction of Santa Trinita may have been begun.

The builders of Trinita IV also introduced a novel element into the elevation: the last chapel on either side is open toward both the side aisle and the transept (Figs. 6, 7), a kind of transposition of the Loggia del Bigallo idea into a church interior.[182] The deceptive simplicity of this innovation does not detract from its architectural significance. The abrupt contrast between the Romanesque rhythm of the nave and the airy width of the transept is mitigated and a subtle transition achieved. It is possible to get an almost complete view of the lower part of the transept from the third nave bay through this device (Fig. 5). As one approaches it, the transept becomes gradually visible in its total height and width. Are we mistaken in recognizing in this gradual revelation of the total space, based on a dynamic conception of the beholder as a figure in motion, the very core of fourteenth century architectural thought? A similar visual experience is repeated in such diverse and yet characteristically late Gothic buildings as Santa Maria del Fiore and the Franziskanerkirche in Salzburg where the Romanesque nave, massive and dim, opens into the bright, centralized space of Stethaimer's early fifteenth century choir.

The question of the architect or architects of Trinita IV must be approached by reviewing the major masters active in Florence in the second half of the fourteenth century.

Francesco Talenti and Giovanni di Lapo Ghini, the *capomaestri* of the *opera del duomo* found themselves partially displaced in the early 1360's by a number of masters, most of them apparently drawn from the *fabbrica* of Santa Maria Novella where vaulting problems had been dealt with since the end of the thirteenth century. This rising group had been active on various Florentine projects since the 1340's. Most important among them are Andrea di Cione, called Orcagna, and Neri di Fioravante. Neri was evidently a personal friend of Orcagna, since he was his witness when Andrea was matriculated into the masons' guild in 1352.[183] The work at Or San Michele, where Orcagna is listed as *capudmagister*,[184] involved vaulting. While Orcagna's main specialty was prob-

---

a pier for fresco left striplike intervening zones. After Castellazzi had washed away all traces of surviving frescoes together with the Baroque plaster over them, these "strips" apparently gave him the *spunto* for his bars. Not one of these strips is original. There is no reason to consider them as a reproduction of the original state, as Paatz has (v, pp. 263, 279, 345 n. 162) and they have no parallel in Florence. Concerning the white stripes on the archivolts, cf. Paatz v, p. 278.

182. For the Oratorio del Bigallo cf. Saalman, "Bigallo."

183. K. Frey, *Die Loggia dei Lanzi zu Florenz*, p. 102.

184. The objections raised against "Orcagna Architetto" at Or San Michele and elsewhere, first by Karl Frey (*Loggia dei Lanzi*, pp. 104f.) and later by Miss Steinweg (K. Steinweg, *Andrea Orcagna*, Strasbourg, 1929, p. 45), Signorina Tosi (L. M. Tosi, "Andrea Orcagna Architetto," *Boll. d'Arte*, XXVII, 1933-1934, pp. 522f.) and Paatz (I, pp. 482, 510 n. 23) are based less on a misreading of the documents than on a misconception of the function of the architect and the architectural process in the 14th century. Although Gaye's interpretation of the documents, on the basis of which he saw Orcagna as *capomaestro* at Or San Michele in the years 1355-1357 (*op.cit.*, I, p. 52), rests on shaky ground, the fact remains that Orcagna was experienced in the basic architectural problems of the period, foundations and vaulting, as evidenced by his consultative role at the cathedral (cf. note 185 infra). Miss Steinweg's suggestion that Orcagna was consulted only regarding questions of internal decoration at

the cathedral (K. Steinweg, "Orcagna," Thieme-Becker, *Künstlerlexikon*, XXVI, Leipzig, 1932, p. 38) is not borne out by the documents. Orcagna is once listed with Taddeo Gaddi and the painters in 1366 (Guasti, *op.cit.*, doc. 141), but usually with the *magistri* (Guasti, docs. 142, 143, 155), although he is sometimes identified as "Andrea pictor" (e.g., Guasti, doc. 154). Cf. also K. Frey's interesting comments (*Loggia dei Lanzi*, pp. 104f.). Frey compares Orcagna's job at Or San Michele and Orvieto with Giovanni Fetti's at the Florentine cathedral in the 1370's. But the fact is that Giovanni *was* capomaestro, even though he was a specialist in sculptural work. On the other hand, even if Orcagna *was* chief master of the entire Or San Michele workshop in the 1350's and not just of the tabernacle (and this is very likely in view of his identical capacity in Orvieto; but cf. M. L. Tosi, *op.cit.*, pp. 518ff.), this does not necessarily mean that there was a design. None of the documents mentions a drawing or a model. When Orcagna entered the Or San Michele workshop in the 1350's, the piers were already finished, but the building begun in 1337 was unvaulted (cf. Paatz IV, pp. 482f. and pp. 511f. n. 24, with a discussion of various attributions). It is a question whether a "design" beyond full-scale *modani* for the piers and details was needed for an open loggia of this kind. The overall measurements could have been and probably were fixed in a written specification. With the plan fixed and the elevation more or less tied to a specific program, all further "design" decisions could be and probably were made as they arose. This is where Orcagna, *Oratorii*

ably sculpture, he was on a commission which had to advise on vaulting problems at Santa Maria del Fiore in 1366, together with Neri di Fioravante.[185]

Neri first achieved prominence in 1340 when he was awarded the commission to construct the great vaults in the hall of the Bargello (Fig. 71).[186] Neri and his associate, Benci Cioni, were also connected with the *opera* of Or San Michele, for which they began the church of San Michele Vecchio (now San Carlo Borromeo) in 1349.[187] Neri's activities are also documented at Santissima Annunziata, where he built the large Falconieri Chapel in 1350, executed various parts of the cloister, and "measured" the church in 1364.[188]

In 1366 Neri was head of a group that formulated a new project for the completion of Santa Maria del Fiore. The project involved an enlargement of the projected octagon and introduction of a drum between the piers and the cupola. It was accepted in 1367 after much discussion.[189]

One significant fact emerges from this survey: in the 1350's and sixties Neri di Fioravante and the group around him, all of them at some time probably connected with or coming from the *fabbrica* of Santa Maria Novella, were in the ascendancy on the Florentine architectural scene. With the final acceptance of the cathedral project in 1367 their triumph was complete.[190] The date of Neri's death is not documented, but his name is last mentioned in 1369 in connection with work at Santissima Annunziata.[191] His associates, Benci Cioni and Francesco Salvetti, held leading posts in the *opera* of Santa Maria del Fiore in the 1370's, and Benci ended his career as one of the chief masters active in the final completion of Or San Michele and the building of the Loggia de' Signori, together with Francesco Talenti's capable son, Simone di Francesco.[192]

Neri's name was first attached to the new Santa Trinita project by Carlo Botto.[193] Botto hinted at indirect evidence in the cloister documents supporting his suggestion and promised a detailed study of Neri's work, which, unfortunately, has never appeared. Paatz repeated Botto's idea without objection, but also without enthusiasm, since for him the entire original project went back to Nicola Pisano.[194] Taucci[195] appears to accept the attribution to Neri as a proven fact.

One thing seems certain. Trinita IV is a product of the Florentine mid- and later fourteenth century. Masters from the leading architectural group of the period, dominant at Santa Maria del Fiore, probably began it, and the group around Simone di Francesco Talenti almost certainly continued it. The resemblance of the transept head console (Fig. 56) to work on the Porta della Mandorla done in the 1390's (cf. note 125) suggests, finally, that the masters around Giovanni d'Ambrogio, *capomaestro* of the Cathedral from 1400 to 1418, finished it.

archimagister (inscription on the tabernacle, dated 1359), played his role. The building is charming in detail and *in toto*, but whether it required "architectural conception" in the conventional sense is another matter altogether. For a recent discussion of this problem and bibliography, cf. the author's "Early Renaissance Architectural Theory and Practice in Antonio Filarete's Trattato di Architettura," ART BULLETIN, XLI, 1959, pp. 89-106.

185. C. Guasti, *op.cit.*, p. 168, doc. 143; cf. Saalman, "Santa Maria del Fiore," p. 484 n. 54.

186. W. Paatz, "Bargello," p. 30.

187. Cf. Paatz I, pp. 411f.

188. Paatz I, pp. 64-65, 74. Benci was called in for advice concerning the Cathedral of Siena in 1358 together with

Francesco Talenti. His written opinion is preserved among the documents in the *opera* of Santa Maria di Siena. Cf. V. Lusini, *Il Duomo di Siena*, I, Siena, 1911, p. 180.

189. Saalman, "Santa Maria del Fiore," pp. 483ff.

190. See note 189.

191. A. Sabatini, "La chiesa della SS. Annunziata di Firenze prima della ricostruzione Michelozziana," *Rivista d'Arte*, XXII, 1940, p. 243.

192. K. Frey, *Loggia dei Lanzi*, p. 106.

193. Botto, 1938, p. 22.

194. Paatz V, p. 327 n. 39.

195. Padre R. Taucci, *La chiesa e il convento della SS. Annunziata di Firenze e i loro amplimenti fino alla metà del secolo XV*, Florence, 1942, p. 18.

Rising Masonry and Foundations

The following brief descriptions summarize our observations concerning the various masonry types encountered on the Santa Trinita site.

TRINITA I

Rising Masonry: Irregular, rather roughly cut blocks (Figs. 11, 19) of *pietra forte*, the standard Florentine masonry granite quarried in the nearby mountains. The sizes vary from 6 x 17cm to 70 x 33cm with medium-sized blocks of roughly 40 x 20cm predominating. The height of the courses runs from 16.5 to 30cm with average heights between 17 and 22cm. The mortar joints were largely refurbished during the nineteenth century restorations. There are no indications that the wall was originally plastered.

Foundations: None. The red clay group is rippled, apparently due to repeated inundations. The rising masonry is set directly on the ground, conforming to the irregularities. Hence, it continues under the pavement line at certain points, but not at others (Fig. 19).

TRINITA IIa

Rising Masonry: Very smoothly worked *pietra forte* ashlars averaging 15 x 40cm with very rare higher blocks up to 30cm (Figs. 9, 25, 26). The blocks are carefully laid in regular courses with fine joints averaging 1-2cm. The side-aisle end wall uncovered in excavation C and left exposed in the space next to the northern trefoil pier in front of Trinita I (Fig. 26) corresponds exactly to that visible in the lower, i.e., Trinita II part of the exposed interior façade. The rising masonry of the *casa solariata* wall is essentially identical with that of Trinita II. It begins at the same ground level, —1.50m (Figs. 34, 35).

Foundations: The Trinita II side-aisle end wall in excavation C under the ground level —1.50m was lined on its eastern side by the side walls of the apparently later tombs, irregularly composed of material probably taken from the now totally demolished Trinita side wall. Since these graves went to a depth of over 3m and it was unfeasible to excavate under the semicircular steps, there was, unfortunately, no opportunity to study the nature of the Trinita IIa foundations within the limits of our excavation. In contrast to the walls of Santi Apostoli and the Baptistery,[196] the

casa solariata wall rests on a crude river-stone and mortar foundation (Fig. 34).

TRINITA IIb

The masonry of the wall closing the spandrel between Trinita I and the Trinita IIa end wall varies from blocks of about 5 x 50cm to blocks of 30 x 65cm with long rather thin blocks predominating. It is set rather carelessly in thick, irregular mortar joints. Extensive plaster remains indicate that this wall was originally plastered (Figs. 30, 31).

There is a roughly 5-10cm projection at the —1.46m level. Under this level the wall continues to a depth of over 3m, i.e., the original ground level of Trinita I. It is difficult to say whether the masonry under —1.46m should be considered rising masonry or foundation since it cannot be stated with certainty whether the ground around Trinita I was raised together with that of Trinita II, or whether the level dropped down sharply around the lower church in order to leave the "crypt" windows exposed.

TRINITA III

With the exception of the upper part of the exposed interior façade (Figs. 9, 10), all surviving Trinita III masonry is part of the foundations (Figs. 37-40). It consists of regularly cut granite blocks averaging 12-15cm in height and 25-30cm in length with occasional blocks up to 30 x 65cm. The joints average 3.5-4.5cm. The blocks are cut roughly even, but not finished smooth. Some smooth-cut blocks may be spoils from another building, perhaps the previous eleventh century church. The practice of reusing demolished masonry in new foundations is documented elsewhere in Florence.[197] There are rare instances of small, thin bricks, not found in earlier masonry.

The masonry of the upper part of the interior façade is smoother than the foundations, but in contrast to the Trinita II stonework below and like the Trinita III foundations, it is an irregular mixture of larger and smaller blocks.

TRINITA IV

Early Phase: We have presented the reasons for considering the clerestory masonry over the second and

196. E. Galli, "Dove sorse 'il bel San Giovanni'," *Rivista d'Arte*, IX, 1916-1918, pp. 81-120, 161-217. Cf. W. Horn, "Das florentiner Baptisterium," *Mitt. Kunsthist. Inst. Florenz*, V, 1938, pp. 100-151. The masonry of the outer foundation wall (cf. Horn, *op.cit.*, p. 142) does not appear to differ significantly from that of the inner wall. There is no reason to connect the outer wall with the documented but wholly undetermined "Lombard" building on the site. K. J. Conant

(*Carolingian and Romanesque Architecture, 800 to 1200*, pp. 230-231) persists in maintaining a late antique origin for the structural fabric of the Baptistery. Santi Apostoli: L. Zumkeller, *Atti della Società Colombaria, Firenze*, X, 1931, pp. 100f.; Paatz I, pp. 226f.

197. For example, at Santa Maria del Fiore; cf. Guasti, *op.cit.*, p. 109.

third southern bays (Fig. 59) as "earlier" in relation to that of the remainder of the structure. This masonry is built up of regular courses with the block length varying from roughly 15-45cm. The course heights run from an average of about 10cm up to 16-20cm in the lower courses of the side-aisle roof line. The joints average 1-2cm. Regularly spaced scaffolding holes remain visible since the exterior was left unplastered. The ashlars of the window jambs are carefully worked without, however, presenting a marked contrast with the adjacent masonry courses other than a contrast of sizes. The jambs of the two windows in this section average 16 blocks with 15 to the arch.

Later Phase: The masonry of all other parts of the church, i.e., the remainder of the clerestory and all visible masonry around the transept and the transept chapels with the exception of modern restorations (see below) is of markedly different character. Regular courses of squared ashlars are abandoned in favor of irregular courses of arbitrarily squared blocks of varying sizes. Whereas the neatly pointed blocks of the early phase presented a relatively rough texture, the masonry of the later phase (Figs. 60, 62) is brought to a smooth facing by a liberal application of mortar. Accordingly it presents a rather lighter coloring compared with the earlier section, which consists in the main of green-grey *pietra forte* mixed with occasional light blocks of *alberese*. The ashlars of the splayed window jambs are somewhat larger than in the early phase, averaging 11-13 blocks to the jamb and 13 blocks to the arches. Since the jamb and arch blocks are more carefully pointed than the surrounding masonry, they present a distinct color contrast with the wall in which they are set. This seems to be a calculated effect.

The east wall of the southern transept arm has two different masonry zones (Fig. 61) which may but need not necessarily indicate successive building periods. Beginning on a level with the springing point of the arch of the large, pointed bifora window and running up to the roof line, we find a crudely coursed masonry. Its main difference from the lower part of the wall is that even the effort of bringing the wall to a smooth

facing by mortar smearing was considered unnecessary. It represents an effort to finish the building as quickly as possible rather than a basic change of technique. It is also noteworthy that the width of the corner buttress was reduced to a slim rib from the same level upward. Since the springing point of the vaults is roughly on a level with the lower line of the large window, the undiminished upward extension of the large pier would have represented a useless expenditure of material and effort. It may be observed in this connection that a similar though, to be sure, much less obvious reduction in the buttress diameter can be noted in the corner piers at Santa Maria Novella (Fig. 67). There too the change may indicate standard masonry practice rather than two distinct building periods.[198]

Later Additions and Restorations: While the bell tower was probably built immediately after the church was completed, it is not an organic part of the building (Fig. 64). Its masonry is a patchwork of a crudity even surpassing that of the later parts of the church and rather characteristic of the Florentine early fifteenth century, when surfaces that were meant to be seen were plastered and whitewashed.

At an indeterminate date after the completion of the building, a buttress was built on either side of the clerestory over the transverse arch between the third and fourth side-aisle bay, apparently to counteract possible signs of buckling in the clerestory wall (Figs. 57, 62).

The report of the subcommission of 1885 noted that round windows had been inserted in the first southern and first and second northern clerestory bays. This may have been done sometime in the sixteenth to eighteenth centuries. These windows were demolished and pointed windows were restored. The masonry of these bays is clearly modern. The subcommission also recommended repairs to the vaults and roof. In connection with this work, 90cm of masonry just under the nave roof line was demolished and renewed, probably to give firmer support to the new roof beams (Figs. 58, 59). This repair was not carried out under the eaves of the transept roof.

198. Cf. note 179 supra.

Membra Disiecta

Since the ground has been repeatedly disturbed in almost all parts of the church by the insertion of tombs and the raising and lowering of the pavement, little material of archaeological value was to be expected remaining loose *in situ*. The finds are, in fact, so meager as to require only brief discussion.

During the repaving work in the "crypt," sherds from several unpainted and unglazed earthenware amphorae were found about 40cm under the pavement level. Identical fragments were unearthed at the —3.00m level in excavation C in the northern side aisle. The vessels had twin handles, a wide opening and nipple bottom (Figs. 75, 76). They may be dated in the late antique period of the city and may indicate the existence of pottery shops on the river banks whose smooth red clay soil supplied the necessary raw material.[199]

A small (ca. 5 x 7cm) mosaic fragment with white, black and grey tesserae was found during our excavations in the southern side aisle in October, 1957 (Fig. 74). Its position in the upper fill makes further deductions useless. The pattern could not be distinguished. It should be noted that the sizable mosaic fragment found during the clearing of the "crypt" in 1885,[200] now in the Museo Nazionale (Bargello), and usually dated in the eleventh century, also consisted of black, white and grey tesserae.

The fill everywhere was abundant in brick fragments (probably the remnants of an older pavement preceding the modern pavement), skeletal remains, traces of nearly decomposed wood and metal (traces of coffins), ceramic fragments of relatively recent date (seventeenth-eighteenth century) and minute fresco fragments. A fairly large piece of worked sandstone appears to be a fragment of a fluted pilaster, perhaps of the fifteenth century and possibly part of a demolished altar ensemble.

Of slightly greater interest is a group of six fragments of *verde di Prato* blocks, originally encrusted with a pattern of pointed shields (probably in marble) (Fig. 77). While all of the encrusted shields had been removed from these blocks, two pieces of marble encrustation of quatrefoil shape and corresponding size, but without matching *verde di Prato* blocks, were also found in the same fill. Fifteen centimeters wide with the shields measuring 11 x 7.5cm, these blocks may be compared with similar blocks now in the pavement of the Chiostro degli Aranci at the Badia with nearly identical patterns though of somewhat smaller dimension. Paatz and Middeldorf[201] have suggested that these blocks came from the pavement of the Gothic Badia and should be dated in the later thirteenth century. Their deduction, though not certain, may nonetheless be justified. For the same reasons, the position of these pieces in the fill under the present pavement does not prove that our blocks are actually from Santa Trinita. On the other hand, it is hard to see why pieces of this kind should have been brought in as fill. They may, indeed, represent the remains of an encrustation pavement of either Trinita III or IV or, more likely, part of the surrounding of a tombstone, which was lifted in the early nineteenth century. The intact blocks were probably removed while the blocks broken during the demolition were discarded into fill after the encrustation had been hacked out.

Two almost completely decomposed copper crucifixes, probably of seventeenth century date, were found in the fill of one of the brick tombs near the *casa solariata* wall.

---

199. Similar sherds have been discovered elsewhere in Florence at the same level, e.g., at San Giovanni (cf. note 196 supra).

200. Paatz V, pp. 268, 339 n. 117.
201. U. Middeldorf and W. Paatz, "Badia," p. 501.

ILLUSTRATIONS

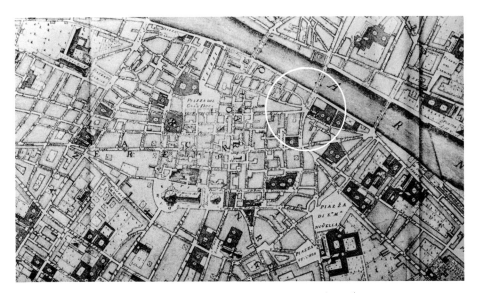

1. Plan of Florence, Ferdinando Ruggieri, 1731 (detail). Santa Trinita in circle

2. View of Piazza Santa Trinita toward Ponte Santa Trinita. At right, the church of Santa Trinita. Directly behind, Palazzo Gianfigliazzi. At left, Palazzo Spini-Ferrari. State 1964 (photo: Phyllis Dearborn Massar)

3. Domenico Ghirlandaio, Santa Trinita, Sassetti Chapel, *Miracle of Saint Francis*, Fresco, 1479-1486 (photo: Alinari)

5. Santa Trinita, Interior toward transept (photo: Phyllis Dearborn Massar)

4. Detail of Fig. 3 (photo: Brogi)

6. Santa Trinita, Interior across nave
(photo: Phyllis Dearborn Massar)

7. Santa Trinita, View into northern transept arm. At lower left, entrance to sacristy (Ghiberti-Michelozzo circle). Center, passage to Via del Parione. At right rear, Ardinghelli Chapel (1393) (photo: Phyllis Dearborn Massar)

8. Santa Trinita, Interior toward façade
(photo: Phyllis Dearborn Massar)

9. Santa Trinita, Interior façade (photo: Alinari)

10. Santa Trinita, Upper part of interior façade (Trinita III period). At left, Trinita III oculus. Indentations at right mark upward extension of Trinita II clerestory. Note contrasting Trinita II and III masonry

11. Santa Trinita, "Crypt," General view north (photo: Phyllis Dearborn Massar)

13. Santa Trinita, "Crypt" stairway. Enclosure designed by Arch. Guido Morozzi, 1957-1958

12. Santa Trinita, "Crypt," view west (photo: Soprintendenza alle Gallerie)

14. Santa Trinita, "Crypt" stairway, view northeast

15. Santa Trinita, "Crypt," view east toward Trinita II pilaster and trefoil pier

16. Detail of Fig. 15. Note junction of relaid Trinita I blocks under Trinita II trefoil pier and Trinita IIb "crypt wall"

17. Detail of Fig. 16 during excavation

18. Santa Trinita, view of eastern "crypt" wall during excavations. Note exposed lower step of original Trinita IIa stairway to Trinita I with Trinita IIb "crypt wall" over it. Traces at top of step mark line of pre-1957 composition pavement and original Trinita I level, —2.97m

19. Santa Trinita, "Crypt," view toward southwest Trinita I wall during pavement demolition. Note irregular foundations

20. Santa Trinita, "Crypt," northern Trinita IV pier foundation at juncture with Trinita I northern apse

21. Santa Trinita, Trinita I window bars removed during 1957 demolitions. Note original Trinita IIb crypt colonette capital fragments in background

22. Santa Trinita, northern Trinita IIa trefoil pier adjoining Trinita I. Note the different *spolia* bases and the Trinita IIb curving steps imposed at right. The retaining wall at right and the stone cover above as well as the concrete pavement in foreground are modern. The base fragment at left was removed from the northern half column of the northern trefoil pier, apparently during the XIX cent. excavations

23. Santa Trinita, southern Trinita II trefoil pier. Retaining wall at left, pavement and covering are modern. Upper part of Trinita IIb "crypt wall" at right restored. In foreground, fragment of original crypt colonette

24. Santa Trinita, view of excavation C toward fourth northern Trinita IV nave pier. At left, Trinita IIb steps (1092f.) adjoining Trinita IIa side aisle end wall (ca. 1060). At right, Trinita IIb spandrel closing wall

25. Santa Trinita, view of Trinita IIb steps and IIa end wall. Note packed mortar and rubble fill in spandrel between IIa end wall and Trinita I conch wall under Trinita IV pier above

26. Santa Trinita, Trinita IIa side aisle end wall adjoining northern trefoil pier on the north. In foreground, fragment of semicircular Trinita IIb steps to choir over crypt

27. Santa Trinita, Excavation C toward southeast. Note intact Trinita II composition pavement east of steps. At left, XVII cent. brick tomb. Curving stone wall behind steps is modern retaining wall around southern Trinita II trefoil pier

28. Santa Trinita, detail of Trinita II composition pavement, originally covered by now missing part of lowermost semicircular step, visible in foreground

30. Santa Trinita, Excavation C from northwest. Spandrel closing wall (IIb) at right

29. Santa Trinita, Excavation C (early phase) toward north. Note modern brick arch closing wall under Trinita IV (modern) chapel steps at rear. In foreground left, Trinita IIa rising end wall continued up to steps by Trinita III (?) end wall foundation (note irregular masonry in contrast to regular Trinita II masonry)

32. Santa Trinita, Excavation C. In foreground Trinita IIa side aisle end wall. Center, IIb spandrel closing wall. Late phase of excavations

31. Detail of Fig. 30, late phase of excavations. Note setback at level −1.46m and rainwater pipe curving off toward north at level −1.51m

33. Santa Trinita, test excavation near southern façade portal. Dislocated portal fragments incorporated in later tomb extending under interior façade wall. In rear, brick and stone foundation wall of Buontalenti façade (1592f.).

34. Santa Trinita, "casa solariata" wall from the west at junction with Trinita III foundation wall (left). Note rubble foundation beginning at level —1.50m

35. Santa Trinita, junction of Trinita III northern side foundation wall (left) with "casa solariata" wall

36. Santa Trinita, continuation of "casa solariata" wall seen from east

38. Detail of Fig. 37. Trinita III southern foundation wall masonry. Note occasional small bricks

37. Santa Trinita, Excavation A (October 1957), general view. Trinita III foundation wall visible under steps

39. Santa Trinita, Excavation D, general view from east

41. Santa Trinita, Excavation F. Southern end of Trinita III period wall under choir chapels. Note that XIV cent. wall above continues on its own foundations at right

43. Santa Trinita, fragment of Trinita III portal. Note projecting piece of lintel. Jamb at left was narrowed when Buontalenti portal was inserted (1592)

40. Santa Trinita, Trinita II foundation wall at junction with "casa solariata" wall seen from the east. Smooth surface at lower right is plaster brick wall closing former breach in foundation wall

42. Santa Trinita, southeast corner of Trinita IV. Note head console in corner. Trinita III round façade window at left, overlapped by Trinita IV arcade pilaster

44. Santa Trinita, Trinita III portal jamb fragment (detail). Late XII–early XIII cent.

45. Santa Trinita, Head console, southeast corner (photo: Alinari)

46. Santa Trinita, Head console, northeast corner (photo: Kunsthistorisches Institut, Florence)

47. Santa Trinita, Pilaster capital between third and fourth southern side chapels, partly restored

48. Florence, Palazzo del Podestà (Bargello), upper loggia. Capital at left, 1332-1346; at right, 1316-1320

49. Santa Trinita, Pilaster capital, first southern arcade pier from east

50. Santa Trinita, Pilaster capital, second southern arcade pier from east

51. Santa Trinita, Vault console capital between second and third southern side chapels

52. Santa Trinita, Pilaster capital between first and second northern side chapels

53. Santa Trinita, Vault console capital between first and second northern side chapels

54. Santa Trinita, Pilaster capital, fifth southern arcade and crossing pier from south (Cf. Fig. 6)

55. Santa Trinita, Nave vault pilaster capital, northern side between first and second bay

56. Santa Trinita, Head console under vault rib, southwestern corner of transept, ca. 1400. Circle of Giovanni d'Ambrogio

57. Santa Trinita, Façade and clerestory, from southeast

59. Santa Trinita, southern clerestory, second and third bays

58. Santa Trinita, southern clerestory, first and second bays

60. Santa Trinita, southern clerestory, second to fifth bays

61. Santa Trinita, southern transept arm from east

62. Santa Trinita, northern clerestory from west

63. Santa Trinita, Choir chapel and
campanile from west (photo: Soprintendenza
alle Gallerie)

64. Santa Trinita, Campanile from north.
Note Donatellesque relief

65. Florence, Porta Romana, 1328

66. Florence, third city wall near Porta Romana,
ca. 1328 (detail)

67. Florence, Santa Maria Novella, Choir chapel,
late XIII cent.

68. Florence, Badia, seen from Via Ghibellina, late XIII cent.

69. Florence, Palazzo del Podestà (Bargello), Courtyard from east

70. Florence, Palazzo del Podestà (Bargello), Façade in
Via Ghibellina from east

71. Florence, Palazzo del Podestà (Bargello), Great Hall, ca. 1250.
Vaults by Neri di Fioravante and Benci di Cione, 1344

72. Florence, San Miniato, Cellar room under sacristy (XIV cent.) facing north. Cellar vaults adjoin crypt wall (XI cent.)

73. Florence, San Miniato, southern side-aisle wall from west

74. Mosaic fragment, found during 1957-1958 Santa Trinita excavations

75. Amphora handle, found during 1957-1958 Santa Trinita excavations

76. Amphora fragment, found during 1957-1958 Santa Trinita excavations

77. *Verde di Prato* incrustation fragments, found during 1957-1958 Santa Trinita excavations

79. Santa Trinita, Section facing south, Castellazzi restoration project including Buontalenti high altar and choir (now in San Stefano al Ponte)

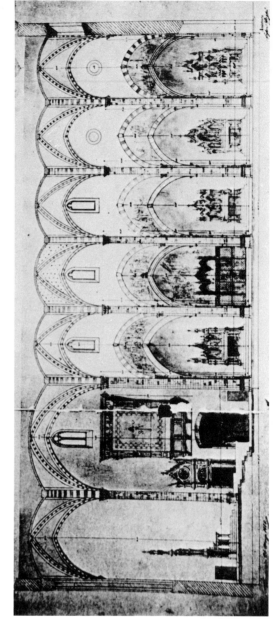

80. Santa Trinita, Section facing south, Castellazzi restoration project (1885) with old organ

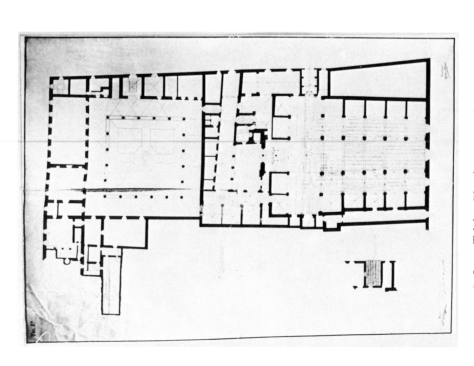

78. Santa Trinita, Plan by G. Castellazzi during restorations of 1885